WARNING!

*Family Vacations May Be
Hazardous to Your Health*

by

Mary Clare Lockman

Beaver's Pond Press, Inc.

Edina / Minnesota

ISBN 1-59298-049-X

Library of Congress Catalog Number: 2003116170

Cover illustration by Hal Rimes
Interior design by Rachel Holscher
Typesetting by Stanton Publication Services, Inc.

Printed in the United States of America

First Printing: February 2004

07 06 05 04 03   6 5 4 3 2 1

Beaver's Pond Press, Inc.

7104 Ohms Lane, Suite 216
Edina, MN 55439-2129
(952) 829-8818
www.BeaversPondPress.com

To order, visit www.BookHouseFulfillment.com or call
1-800-901-3480. Reseller discounts available.

Dedication

To my traveling companions.
Mary Ann: Thank you for everything.
Anne, Clare, Erin, Colleen: I love being your mom.
Paul: You still make me laugh after all these years.
I love all of you.

Enjoy! :)
Mary Clare
Lockman

Acknowledgements

I wish to thank my friend, Marne McLevish, for adding the word "Warning" to the title. Thank you to Cindy Rogers for her editing help. Thank you to all the people who answered my e-mails and sent me information. The Laura Ingalls Wilder Memorial Society was very helpful. Thank you. The Mitchell Area Chamber of Commerce was a wonderful resource. Thank you. The United States Department of the Interior National Park Service sent me amazing, interesting packets of information. Thank you. The Smithsonian people write the nicest e-mails ever. Thank you. Thank you to Rachel Holscher for her expertise in design. And, of course, thank you very much to Milt Adams for helping my dream become a reality.

Contents

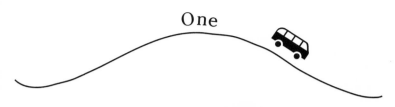

Welcome to the Parlor

*Beware of the parlor, where children put on
their best clothes and their best faces.*

During the inky-black winter of 1985, my husband, Paul, and I meticulously planned our trip to Yellowstone National Park. As afghans swaddled the two of us, we poured through guide books, perused maps, discussed pros and cons of local attractions, and booked motel reservations. While we slept, we dreamed of what was sure to be the perfect family vacation.

We purchased a van in May with the idea of traveling for many summers to come.

The day of our dreams arrived. On a sunlit morning in June, we left St. Paul, Minnesota, to begin our first driving trip with our three daughters. Anne was six-and-a- half, Clare was four, and Erin was two-and-a-half. My mother,

Mary Ann, was along also to complete our three generation family.

I was so excited I didn't stop smiling for the first hundred miles.

"Wait a minute. Wasn't that Plum Creek?" I asked. At the entrance to a small bridge was a large sign saying, "Plum Creek." The creek swirled below us for a few seconds and then, it was gone.

"What's Plum Creek?" Paul asked, as we crossed the creek.

"You don't know?" I couldn't believe my ears.

"No. What is it?"

"I thought everybody knew about Plum Creek."

"I don't."

"The Ingalls family lived there in their soddy house. Anne, that was Plum Creek we just went over." I craned my neck to look behind us. The sign, bridge, and creek were getting smaller and smaller.

I had read *Little House in the Big Woods* by Laura Ingalls Wilder to our girls from the time they were toddlers. Anne was now reading the whole series of eight books about the Ingalls family by herself. She loved the stories as much as I had when I was young.

"I loved the soddy house," Anne said. She looked out the back window trying to catch a glimpse of the creek. It had disappeared.

"I thought we were stopping in DeSmet?" Paul asked.

"We are," I said. While curled by the fireplace during

the winter, I had talked Paul into taking a different route and stopping in DeSmet, South Dakota. The last house of the Ingalls family was there.

"Aren't we seeing a house of the Ingalls there?"

"Yes, but they moved a lot. You know; *Little House in the Big Woods, Little House on the Prairie*."

The two lane road stretched in front of us. It was quiet and unhurried, with little traffic. The only sounds were our whirring wheels on the pavement and the whooshing wind against the windows. One last time I looked back in the direction of Plum Creek.

"What's the difference between one house or another?" Paul asked. He had never read the books and knew of them only from me reading to the girls.

"They're all very different. Aren't they, Anne?"

Anne nodded in agreement.

"The soddy house was always my favorite of their houses. I didn't know we were going right by it," I said.

We were now a couple of miles past Plum Creek. "Anne, was Nellie Oleson in the Plum Creek story?" I twisted my head so I could see Anne.

"I think so. Ooh, I hated Nellie."

"She wasn't very nice in the book, was she?"

"Sometimes Laura did things too."

"Yes, she did. Oh well, no kid is perfect."

Paul pulled over to the side of the road and stopped. "Do you want to stop here?"

"Sure. Do you want to, Anne?"

"Sure."

"Clare and Erin, do you want to?" I asked.

"I do," Clare said. Clare had been listening to the back and forth without making a sound. That was more than an unusual occurrence; it was downright astonishing. She liked to make her viewpoints known on every subject. If no one shared her views, Clare just planted her sturdy self, wherever she was, and didn't move, physically or mentally.

"Me too," Erin squeaked. Erin had a fragile, almost spindly body. And her voice was as long and skinny as her limbs.

"Mom, do you want to stop?" I asked Grandma.

"Whatever you and Paul want," Grandma said.

"We can't stop here and DeSmet," Paul said. "It'll get too late." Paul had planned for the driving to end each day at five o'clock at the latest.

"Where are we staying tonight?" I asked.

"Mitchell."

"Is that far from DeSmet?"

"About two hours."

"That's pretty far. I don't want to be too late either." I had to agree we couldn't see everything but I didn't like missing Plum Creek.

"I don't care one way or another," Paul added.

"I'd guess I'd rather stop in DeSmet. That's where *The Long Winter* took place."

"Does everyone agree?" Paul asked.

I nodded my head. There was a general consensus

coming from the back of the van. Our five-minute discussion over, we were back on the two lane highway heading for DeSmet, South Dakota.

DeSmet was the last town the Ingalls family lived in. In addition to that, it was also the place where Laura Ingalls had taught school.

Our first stop was the tiny school, a replica of the original school called the Brewster School. It was named after the Brewster family, whose children were three of Laura's five students. She taught one term of school there while living with the Brewster family.

We opened the door and walked into the back of the schoolroom. The teacher's desk sat squarely in front of the class. Behind it a blackboard covered the wall. In the corner, a coal burning stove squatted, ready and waiting for winter. Adding the four double desks for students filled the room.

We walked around the one-room schoolhouse taking in everything from the slate boards to the primers on each desk. A large map of the United States hung on the side wall. I tried to imagine children walking miles to school during their long, cold winters.

Tour guides were available in the school and house. They were elated that we had read all the books. "You've read all the books. Wonderful!" The tour guide's hands embraced each other as she exclaimed. "Wonderful!" She looked at each of us with a huge smile.

After the schoolhouse visit, we drove to the last house the Ingalls had lived in. A guide met us as we stepped through the door.

"Come in. Welcome," she said.

She first told the story of the family as they were portrayed in the books. Then she talked about what brought the family to DeSmet, and finally the building of the house. As she spoke of the Ingalls family, her eyes shone with passion.

The guide relished questions of all kinds, especially from the children. Anne, my mother, and I were interested in what happened to Laura and her sisters later in their lives.

"Did Laura live here?" Anne asked.

"No, she never lived in this house. The family moved in after Laura was married."

We learned that the family had come to DeSmet when Laura was twelve. They lived in the Surveyor's House out of town the first year. *By The Shores Of Silver Lake* was written about that area. During *The Long Winter,* the family stayed in town above the store Pa bought.

We also learned sadly that there were no living descendants of Ma and Pa Ingalls.

We knew from the stories how skillful Pa Ingalls was with his hands. This last house of theirs was added on to many times. It even had a parlor.

While the guide pointed out special items, we toured the house. We went first to the upstairs bedrooms. Coming back downstairs, we walked into an attractive kitchen.

We all liked the cupboards because they were made by Pa but we had saved the best for last.

"And now, we can carefully walk into the parlor. Again, don't touch anything," the tour guide stated. She adjusted her white gloves above the elbows. She wore a dress of the late 1800s with skirt and petticoats swishing the floor. The toes of her polished black boots peeked out from under the skirt. Buttons that held the boots together reflected light in waves on their surfaces.

We followed the guide and stepped into a restful, pretty front room. Lace curtains veiled the windows as the sun poured in. Two comfortable-looking chairs sat facing each other, while, nearby, pictures and books stood on wooden tables. Family pictures hung on the walls. Under the portraits of Ma and Pa, a black fainting lounge invited us. It looked like a prime spot to recline and read. Against the opposite wall from Ma and Pa, an aged organ waited with sheet music open.

"Pa made all of this, Anne," I said.

"It's neat. Thank you, Mom and Dad."

"You're welcome." I stole a glance at Paul and knew he was feeling the same way I did. Our hearts swelled with pride. They are so pleasant and appreciative, I thought.

True joys to travel with!

I had driven the van only a few times and wasn't as comfortable with it as my husband. Paul had planned on doing most of the driving on the trip. The first day he had done all of it.

"Wait. What's that big building?" I asked. Our van had just breezed right by an unusual looking building.

"The Mitchell Corn Palace," Paul said.

"Can't we stop?"

"I think we should check in at the hotel before we do anything else."

"What is it? I've read about it."

"It's a building decorated with parts of the corn plant. Maybe we'll want to go back after dinner."

During January, February, and March, I had read about places of interest in South Dakota, Wyoming, and Colorado. The Corn Palace had intrigued me. I couldn't believe what the local people went through to create it each year.

Every September they stripped the walls and started fresh with 275,000 new corn stalks, cobs, grasses, and grains. The cobs were sawed in half and nailed individually to the walls. Eleven different colors were used in the designs; all of them native to South Dakota.

Artists designed the new murals for each year's theme. The outside designs were also made of corn parts and quite intricate. This tribute to agriculture was a true labor of love.

As we drove by, I glimpsed the outside patterns which looked like cowboys riding their horses. At least one of the cowboys had his right hand raised twirling a lasso. So much action was within the designs that I could picture the horses galloping. I could almost hear the cowboys talking to their horses and yelling orders to each other. I tried to imagine the inside of the palace.

I wanted to stop but it had been a long day for all of us. "Are you guys hungry?" I asked. I turned around to the back.

"Yes," the girls answered in unison.

"I am too. Let's eat."

After eating and relaxing for a while no one felt like driving the two miles back to the Corn Palace, including me. The girls swam in the hotel pool with Paul. Grandma and I sat by the pool and talked about our full day.

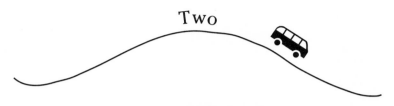

Two

The Wild West

Enjoy today with your children, for
tomorrow may be very different

The next day we stopped at a prairie dog town on the side of the highway. The three girls found out that prairie dogs were impossible to sneak up on. The girls crouched down as they inched forward. If they moved a leg in any direction, the prairie dogs disappeared down a hole. Within seconds, the little prairie dogs popped out of another hole, alert to any movement.

"There it is," Anne yelled. She stooped down, put her finger to her lips, and started to move forward. The prairie dog was already gone.

"I see it," Clare cheered. She put her finger to her lips, and tiptoed ahead.

"Mom, it's a mom," Erin said excitedly. She pointed to a prairie dog followed by smaller versions of itself.

"Kids always follow their moms. Right, Erin?" I asked. I had nicknamed Erin "my little shadow" because every time I turned around she was right there. Her innate shyness meant she didn't want me out of her sight.

We watched as the mother prairie dog ran down the holes with little ones in swift pursuit.

The temperature was in the mid-nineties, Fahrenheit. When the wind burst across the prairie, it was hard to take in a deep breath. I panted with each fiery gust. My sporadic breaths came in spurts, after the blasts of hot air were through. It reminded me of the breathing exercises nurses taught pregnant woman to use during labor. It didn't work out here on the hot prairie, either.

We took a detour off the main highway to view the Badlands. I don't know what I expected, but it certainly wasn't the stark beauty in front of us. The unusual rocky landscape made me feel like we had landed on the moon. There wasn't a plant, tree, bush, or anything green facing us. The slabs of stone and rock looked like stalagmites sticking up from the ground in all directions.

I was surprised how wide the Badlands were. They literally went on for miles and miles. A nearby sign stated that the Badlands area encompassed 379 square miles.

"Isn't it beautiful?" I asked anyone who happened to be listening.

"It's hot everywhere," Clare said. "Really hot."

"Yes, it is," I said. Erin had been standing right next to me. Now she leaned against me. I didn't have the heart to tell her that she was too sweaty for snuggling.

"Do you like it here, Erin?" Paul asked.

"Mm hmm."

"I like it too," he said. He patted her fine, blond hair.

Anne had been standing with her hands on her hips as she gazed out. It lasted for only a second, but I saw it clearly. She narrowed her eyes at Clare and stuck her tongue out so fast, that if I had blinked, I would have missed it. Then she bounced off to the van.

I made a mental note to talk to Paul about what I had seen. We could nip any problems in the bud before they became unmanageable. When I reached the van, I looked in the back and all seemed calm. No problem.

Signs along the highway contained extensive advertising for Wall Drug. Our interest piqued, we invented a game to see who would notice the signs first.

"Would anyone like to stop?" Paul asked.

"I would," I said.

"I would."

"I would."

"I would."

"It would be interesting to actually see Wall Drug," Grandma said. "Especially after seeing all the signs."

We drove to Wall Drug, found one of the few empty parking places, and parked the van. Inside the different rooms, pictures and Western memorabilia decorated the walls. Each room was packed with people; talking, laughing, and eating. Some of the people were eating buffalo burgers and drinking sarsaparilla. A general feeling of happiness and camaraderie pervaded the drugstore. As we listened to the medley of voices, we heard many different languages.

Since I love museums, I was thrilled that Wall Drug had a museum on the premises. It gave an interesting history of South Dakota and, especially, Wall Drug.

It was established in 1931, during the Depression. Business grew tremendously after they offered free ice water to anyone who stopped. Since motor vehicles had no air-conditioning, the ice water tasted great to the hot, thirsty travelers. Fifty years later, the ice water still tasted great.

With the friendly atmosphere, Wall Drug was also the perfect place to buy an ice cream cone. As we licked our cones, and sipped our sarsaparilla, we sat for a long time and watched the people.

Before stopping in Rapid City for the night, we wanted to see Mount Rushmore. It was incredible! We stared at the four chiseled faces of our presidents. A tape recording told us why these four were chosen, as well as how Gutzon Borglum carved the faces.

Borglum felt that Washington, Jefferson, Lincoln, and Teddy Roosevelt signified the tenets of freedom and democracy. George Washington was chosen for being commander of the Revolutionary army and our first president. Thomas Jefferson, our third president, was remembered for writing the Declaration of Independence. Abraham Lincoln, our sixteenth president, was selected for holding the nation together during the Civil War. Borglum chose our twenty-sixth president, Teddy Roosevelt, for his promotion of conservation, business reform, and the construction of the Panama Canal.

Inside, we watched the video of the men who made the monument. With their jack hammers shaking and vibrating, workers were suspended by ropes in front of the mountain. They knocked off certain areas of rock and left other areas intact.

We learned that Borglum had started carving in 1927 and continued until his death in 1941. He persevered throughout the Great Depression. After his death, his son, Lincoln, put the finishing touches on the monument.

"Washington's nose alone is 20 feet long," the tape intoned.

We went outside to see for ourselves.

"Their noses are so big," Clare said. She touched her nose a couple of times, finding it to be quite a bit smaller than the noses before us.

"Look at their noses, Anne," Grandma said.

We were all amazed by the noses. From far away they looked huge, but when we took our turns looking through the viewing telescope, the noses were enormous.

"Let me look," I said. I stared at the 60 feet of granite face, 500 feet above the ground, and zeroed in on Lincoln's nose. I had an instant image of Cary Grant above the presidents in the movie "North By Northwest." I tried to imagine how they shot that scene. I also imagined being in the scene with him, slipping, and Cary Grant catching me. It wasn't an unpleasant fall down that nose at all.

"Mom, it's my turn," Erin said.

I turned over the viewer to my daughter, bounced out of my reverie.

We had been talking up the fact that there would be a swimming pool at the motel. The night before, the girls hadn't stopped swimming until bedtime. We knew the pool was outdoors, but that was fine since it was so hot. We got to the motel, checked in, and then looked around for the pool.

We didn't hear any splashing, gleeful shouts, or any of the other sounds you hear when people are enjoying the water. We were puzzled.

"I'm going to get on my swimming suit right away," Anne said. "Can I, Dad?"

"Sure, as soon as we find the pool."

We drove all the way around the parking area, sure we had missed something. And we had. There was a pool there but no one was swimming in it. There wasn't any water in it!

The motel wasn't air conditioned so we were in a dilemma. Our choices were to sit outside in the heat until we all passed out, or sit in our rooms and pass out on the beds. We brought the luggage into our rooms. Within five minutes, perspiration beaded on our foreheads and noses.

"I wish I could swim," Anne said. She paced around the room.

"It's hot everywhere," Clare said.

"We can't stay here, that's for sure," Paul said.

We decided to look for an air conditioned restaurant and take our time with the meal. We found a McDonald's that was both air conditioned and had a play area. It was perfect. Hamburgers and french fries disappeared quickly.

"Can we go play?" Anne asked.

"Can we?"

"Can we?"

"Sure, go ahead." I said.

Paul, Grandma, and I enjoyed the cool air, the french fries, and the quiet. We talked about what we would do the next day. There were so many parks and activities for families that we had trouble deciding what to do.

We told the girls they could have an ice cream cone before we left McDonald's.

"Thank you, Mom and Dad," Anne said.

"You're the best mom and dad," Clare said.

"Thank you," Erin said as she licked her ice cream.

My pride-filled heart needed a bigger rib cage to expand in. What was the big deal about traveling with kids? It wasn't hard at all. It was a piece of cake!

By the time we got back to the motel, the temperature had cooled. We were all so tired we went to sleep without a problem.

The next morning we drove to a free dinosaur park. The giant heads were visible far in the distance. As soon as the van pulled into a parking place and stopped, the girls raced toward the park.

"Look. There they are," the three girls said in one voice.

The dinosaurs were life-sized reproductions which made them all the more awe-inspiring. The girls ran to each of the five dinosaurs, stood there, and gawked. They perched together on the massive frill of Triceratops. As we stood next to Tyrannosaurus Rex and Brontosaurus, I thanked God that the Age of Dinosaurs was over.

"Look at those teeth," Clare said, pointing to Tyrannosaurus Rex.

"They're six inches long," Paul said.

"Would they chase us?"

"Of course, Clare, and they'd eat us too," Anne said.

Erin moved right next to me. I put my arm around her while I imagined being chased down the streets of St. Paul by those six-inch long, smirking teeth.

Our next stop was Storybook Island. It was also free to the public. All the little scenes were from children's books and rhymes. The whole place had an almost magical feel to it.

One of the things we liked to do at home was act out stories from books. Each girl took a different part. They had lines to remember while Paul or I were the narrators. One of their favorites was *The Three Billy Goats Gruff.*

Anne saw the bridge with the troll underneath first.

"Try to get me, troll," Anne said as she skipped across the bridge. The Billy Goats Gruff were on the other side.

Clare stopped in the middle of the bridge and looked into the troll's eyes. She was ready if he tried to get her.

Clare was the only one who loved to be the troll when we acted out the story.

Erin hesitated. I was just going to tell Erin I would go across with her when her sisters called to her.

"Erin, c'mon," Clare said. "We'll wait for you."

"Yeah, hurry up," Anne said.

"Isn't that nice the way they look out for each other?" I asked Paul and Grandma.

"They've been very good," Grandma said. "Of course, there's plenty for them to see and do."

"It's been much better than I thought it would be," Paul said.

"I'd take them anywhere," I said.

The three girls skipped and laughed as they went from story to story. After a while, they came over to tell us they were done.

Anne said, "Thank you, Mom and Dad."

"You're welcome," I replied. My heart swelled again.

"Thank you, Mom and Dad," Clare said.

"Thank you, Mom and Dad," Erin echoed.

My heart was positively bursting with love for my offspring.

Memories are more unique if they are flavored with variety. I would soon find that our trip would be unforgettable for more reasons than our children bounding with joyfulness.

We had seen signs along the road for a bear park. I had no idea what it was, but I thought it might be interesting for the girls. We decided to drive through after everyone but Anne said they wanted to see bears. Before we knew it, the gate had closed behind us and there was no retreating.

Following a small sports car in front of us, we drove around, peering out the window, looking for bears.

"Look, girls," Paul said, pointing at Rocky Mountain Goats in the distance.

"Aren't they neat?" Grandma said. The goats were so sure-footed on the crags and ledges that they could dash along the uneven rock as if it were a highway.

"They're beautiful," I said.

"How do they run like that?" Anne asked.

"Yeah, how do they run so fast?" Clare asked.

"They hop," Erin said. "Hop, hop." Erin moved her right fingers up and down in her left hand.

We continued to search for bears. To Anne's delight, they proved to be elusive. That is, until we turned the last corner. There were black bears everywhere. They seemed to be intrigued by the cars, especially the little two-seat car we were following. The bears crawled over the hood, the roof, and the trunk of the car. We stopped.

"Don't stop," Anne said.

"We have to," Paul said.

Anne started biting her nails. "What if they try to crawl on us?"

"They can't. The van is too high," I said. To tell the truth, I was getting pretty nervous myself. I hoped the bears weren't interested in us. I wasn't finding them anywhere near as cute as I thought I would. And they certainly weren't cuddly. Their long, sharp claws were poised, ready for anything.

"I don't like bears," Anne said.

"Me too, Anne," Grandma said.

"When can we leave?"

"After the other cars leave, we can go," Paul said.

"Do you think they're scratching that guy's car?" I asked.

"I don't know. It sure looks like it."

The man and the woman in the sports car were having an animated conversation. I figured it was about whose idea it was to drive through the bear park. The sports car inched forward so it wouldn't run over the bears and finally, it was free. The car raced out of the gate, leaving black tire marks on the pavement.

We were next. Paul wasn't taking any chances that the bears would find our van fascinating. He gunned the motor before they could even look us over. We peeled out of there and onto the highway.

"Let's not go back there," Anne said.

"We won't." We all agreed.

As we drove along, we saw a sign stating we were going towards the Needles Highway.

The road narrowed to one lane. I looked at the stone tunnel ahead of us. There was no way the van could fit through.

"We aren't going to make it. The van is too wide," I said.

"We'll fit. You'll see," Paul said as he drove towards the tunnel.

I was glad the tunnel wasn't longer than it was because I was afraid a car would come through from the other direction. After we made it through the tunnel, I exclaimed over the astonishing vistas and views in Custer National Park.

The tall granite spires rose in sharp points towards the sky. One spire called Cathedral Spire was a favorite of mountain climbers.

"Look, there's a hole in the rock," Anne said. She pointed out the window.

"Cool," Clare said.

"It really is cool," I said. The hole in the rock was a natural formation that caused an elongated opening. It looked exactly like an eye of a gigantic needle. "It wouldn't be hard to thread that needle," I said.

"I love that," Grandma said.

The whole flavor of the West was strong as we drove through South Dakota. Along the side of the road ran the ruts from the covered wagons a century before. A hundred years of rain and snow had not erased them. I thought of the people trekking to Oregon so many years before us. How many of them had better lives if and when they reached their destination?

The girls were intrigued most of all by the wildness of the West. They liked the stories of the outlaws and people carrying guns.

We drove to Deadwood, South Dakota to see where Wild Bill Hickock was killed. We walked into Old Style No.10 Saloon.

"Girls, they say this is where Wild Bill Hickock was shot," I said.

"Who was that?" Anne asked.

"A famous lawman of the wild west."

"Were there outlaws too?" Clare asked.

"Lots of them. It really was wild."

"Who else hung around here?" Anne asked.

"I know Calamity Jane did," I said.

We continued to walk towards the back where the poker tables were. I reached down to take Erin's hand. Erin had stayed right next to me in the murkiness of the saloon. A group of people stood around a table where two black eights and two black aces lay face up. Other cards were scattered around.

"This is called the Dead Man's Hand in poker," Paul said.

"Why?" Anne asked.

"Because that's what he was holding when he was shot."

"Cool," Anne and Clare both said.

I thought that was a peculiar response to someone being shot, but I didn't ask for an explanation. Mothers don't need to know everything.

We stayed in Lead, South Dakota, for the night in a quiet two-floor motel.

I wished we could have stayed in the Black Hills area

longer. We didn't even begin to experience it. There were hot springs, caves, and other parks, as well as many places to hike. We needed a full week, but we had made reservations in Yellowstone and the Grand Tetons months before.

We left the Black Hills at eight the next morning, vowing to return soon.

"Goodbye, Black Hills," Clare said.

"Goodbye," Erin said.

We crossed over the border into northeastern Wyoming and followed the signs saying, "Devil's Tower."

The lone stone tower came straight up out of the ground with its clawed out sides and flat mesa top. As with Cathedral Spire, Devil's Tower was a favorite of mountain climbers. I told the girls it was a challenging climb even for experienced mountain climbers. Through the video camera, we zoomed in, looking for climbers in the distance. I wondered how anyone could climb it and then rappel down the sides.

We read that Devil's Tower was thought to be the core of a volcano. Millions of years of erosion exposed the tower to rise more than 1200 feet. In 1906, Teddy Roosevelt dedicated Devil's Tower as the first national monument.

We stayed the night in Sheridan, Wyoming. This time the pool was filled with heated water. It was also indoors, so the girls swam happily until bedtime.

After pajamas were on, I asked the girls what their favorite part of the trip was so far.

"Storybook Island," Erin said excitedly. "And the dinosaurs."

"I thought you were scared of Tyrannosaurus?" Anne asked.

"I was but I still liked them."

"Well, I liked the Ingalls house and the schoolhouse," Anne said.

"What about you, Mom," I asked Grandma.

"It's hard to pick one thing but I loved that eye of the needle," Grandma said.

"I can't decide either. I liked all of the Black Hills," I said.

"I liked Mount Rushmore," Paul said.

"Me too."

Clare had been strangely quiet throughout the exchange.

"What about you, Clare?" Grandma asked.

"I liked Devil's Tower," she said with a glint in her eye. "But I really liked the bears best of all." She smirked at Anne and stuck out her tongue.

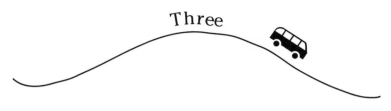

Three

Sisterly Love

*Nothing takes more patience than
riding in a car with children.*

We began the fifth day of our trip excited to see Yellowstone National Park. We planned on arriving in Yellowstone by mid afternoon.

We had replaced our shorts the previous day with jeans and sweaters. We got out our jackets and put them in the back of the van. The temperature was in the mid-thirties, a change of 60 degrees from two days before.

We started to drive through the Bighorn Mountains. I declared each turn to be the most beautiful and then the next curve brought even more splendor. The pristine lakes and the forests against the backdrop of the mountains were awe-inspiring. We stopped to let the girls play in the snow and to gaze at some of the breathtaking scenery. I couldn't get enough of the loveliness surrounding us.

It was slow going around the bends and twists of the road. Earlier, we had discussed going into Montana to see where the Battle of the Little Bighorn took place. As the hours went by, I was glad we hadn't tried to fit that in.

Paul handed the keys to me after seven hours of driving. "I can't drive anymore," he said. "My eyes are so tired they hurt."

"I don't mind driving."

We pulled the van over and switched places. I adjusted mirrors, seat, and the steering wheel. I was set. We were a scant 20 miles from the entrance to Yellowstone.

It was four-thirty in the afternoon. The girls were getting restless. It became impossible for them to sit still. As their bodies wiggled and wriggled, the release of energy came from their vocal cords.

"Would you make them be quiet?" I implored. "I can't drive like this."

"I'm trying," Paul said.

We passed the Eastern entrance to the Park. We were making our way to the Old Faithful Inn, where we planned to spend two nights. The man at the gate said it would be no more than a half hour. We were all relieved the end was in sight. I told the girls it would be 45 minutes at the most.

The two lane highway was narrow and the traffic was heavy. Many large campers, RVs, and buses were coming towards us. There was barely enough room for our van to pass. I felt I had to inch up against the mountain or I'd collide with an RV. As the mountainside swept by the window, I heard a sharp intake of air from my husband. I didn't dare even glance at him; my focus was on the serpentine road ahead of me.

"She's looking at me," Clare shouted.

"No, I'm not. I wouldn't waste my time, Clare," Anne shouted even louder.

"Make her stop," Clare yelled.

The van vibrated with the commotion.

"Mom, are we there?" Erin's high-pitched voice cut through the noise. It always did. It was a mixture of chalk rasping on a blackboard and brakes screeching on the street.

"Mom is trying to drive," Grandma whispered in a voice louder than her normal talking. "Stop it."

Tenacious Clare was not about to give up. "She better stop looking at me," Clare said with her fist raised toward Anne.

"Please get in the back with them," I said to Paul. "Please."

There was nowhere to pull over but I was starting to fear for the safety of my mother. I glanced in the rear-view mirror every couple of seconds. I could see Erin hanging on to her blanket for dear life. In the front with me, Paul stroked his mustache from the middle outward twice per second. His head turned front to back, front to back, as he struggled to watch both the road and the unraveling girls. After I asked him to get in the back, he crawled over the seats and changed places with Grandma.

"Whew," Grandma said as she burrowed into the front seat. "That was something."

It had been over an hour since we went through the entrance to the park. According to the map, we weren't even halfway there. I had a nagging thought that we had ten more days on our trip. As much as I tried to push the thought out of my mind, it kept coming back like the perfect boomerang.

Ten more days. Ten more days.

The fighting continued in the back. I was concentrating so hard on driving that I could tune most of it out.

Paul and I had discussed what we would do about fighting in the van before we left St. Paul. We thought we could handle any fighting that came up by not allowing the child to swim for a half hour when we got to the hotel. I had read about it in a book about parenting and it sounded logical. We told the girls at the beginning of the trip that this would be our punishment for fighting.

We had a different problem now. The places we were staying in for the next five nights didn't have pools. I knew that saying, "Six nights from now you will have to wait a half hour to swim," would not have the calming effect I wanted.

Paul tried to interest Anne and Clare in cards, road games (count the campers), but their hearts weren't in it. They had both found their niche and there was no turning back.

"She bugs me so much!"

I couldn't determine which of the two said it. Their voices had sort of melded together in their shrillness.

The middle of a thunderstorm could not have been more electric.

"Would you two stop?" Paul pleaded.

"I hate her."

"The driving is terrible, girls." One last appeal.

"I hate her, too."

"Nobody hates anyone," I said. I couldn't tune the word hate out. I was going to add that I had never hated anyone when I was interrupted by Anne.

"How do you know?" Anne asked. "I do too hate her."

"No, you don't. She's your sister." The quagmire of our children's fighting was pulling me under.

"SO," Anne and Clare stated passionately.

"Ignore them," Grandma "whispered."

"Easier said than done," I said.

"If you don't quit fighting, I'm going to spank both of you," Paul finally said in a voice as clipped as his mustache.

My mouth opened and then shut tightly.

There was a hushed silence that settled over the van. This had not been part of our original consequences.

We limped into The Old Faithful Inn two and a half hours after entering the park. We were all numb: from sitting, from fighting, from family togetherness. Grandma scurried off for a quick walk. The rest of us trudged inside.

As we opened the door, I exclaimed out loud. It was more like entering a cathedral than a hotel. The wide open center of the century old inn was about five or six stories high. All the supporting structures and beams were of exposed wood. Some beams were entire tree trunks with the bark and branches removed. The openness gave me a sense of freedom, while the warmth of the wood drew me in, welcoming. Interesting-looking shops were located all around the main floor.

We registered at the front desk and brought our luggage to a double room on the third floor. Everything about it was spare and simple. I thought it was perfect. The girls noticed that there wasn't any bathroom in the room. It was down the hall. I assured them that I would be outside the door as a lookout when they showered.

"Mom, Old Faithful is interrupting," Anne said. I quickly went out to the veranda and watched. Old Faithful was about 200 yards away from the Inn. We had a perfect view of the famous geyser as it erupted. Hot water and steam spewed high into the air.

"It's wonderful," I said.

"I'm going to watch it interrupt every hour," Anne said.

"Me too," Clare said.

After the sun went down, the girls put on their pajamas.

Paul, Grandma, and I were drawn to the wooden deck that encircled the entire third floor. Each of the three floor levels had a deck surrounding it. Wooden tables and chairs were scattered throughout. Groups of people sat at the tables drinking, chatting, and looking out at the heart of the Inn.

A piano player sat down at the grand piano on the second floor level. Soon he was playing songs from

Broadway musicals. We sat down at one of the tables to watch and listen.

When the girls heard the music, the three of them came out of the room. They knew most of the songs from our tapes at home. Anne and Clare sat at the table while Erin crawled up on my lap with her blanket. It covered every part of her frail body except her head.

"Do you like it here?" I asked.

"Mm, hmm," Erin said as she snuggled in closer.

A man stood up next to the piano. He began to sing. He had no microphone but he didn't need it for his glorious voice filled every square inch of the huge building. People stopped talking, spellbound. He sang one song after another. We heard the piano play the introduction to "Edelweiss."

"He's going to sing your favorite, Erin," I said.

She already had the dreamy look in her eyes that she always got when she heard "Edelweiss." She put her head on my shoulder and I held her tighter. The song carried us away.

I knew if I lived to be a hundred, and traveled the world over, it would never get better than this.

The next day the girls showered with me as "the lookout." After everyone had finished washing and drying hair, getting dressed, and eating breakfast, we went outside.

The area around Old Faithful had a long boardwalk. A walkway went between the myriad of other geysers and water-filled hot springs. The colors of the water were every shade of blue and blue-green; from aqua, to teal, to the deeper blues. We walked at a leisurely pace because the girls didn't want to miss any geysers. One they all liked was a little bit of water percolating under a couple of pebbles. Erin discovered it after the rest of us had walked by.

"Mom, I found a baby," Erin tweeted.

"Isn't that cute? Look girls."

We wondered if it would get as big as Old Faithful.

In the afternoon we drove to the Grand Canyon of Yellowstone and a place called the Paint Pots. My mother stayed with Erin so they could rest. The Grand Canyon was a deep gorge filled with waterfalls and rushing water. I didn't expect it to be so large and so "grand". The sound and the power of the waterfalls mesmerized me. We drove around to see different views of the canyon. We were wishing—as we had in The Black Hills—that we had a full week to spend in Yellowstone.

Our next stop was the Paint Pots, mud ponds that boiled and bubbled from the heat underneath. A sulfuric smell saturated the air.

"It smells like eggs," Clare said, plugging her nose.

"Yeah, rotten ones," Anne said, sniffing the air.

There were other geysers too; one had been erupting continuously for decades.

For Anne, no other geyser could compare with Old Faithful's "interrupting." "I love Old Faithful the best," Anne said.

"Why don't you marry it then?" Clare asked. This

was Clare's response anytime the word love was used. I was getting "married" several times a day. I loved everything!

We saw elk, buffalo, mountain goats, and other animals. What an unusual place! We returned to the Inn bubbling with things to tell Grandma and Erin.

I'm not much of a shopper but each of the shops I mentioned earlier was owned by an artist. As we walked from shop to shop, the artists painted, sculpted, and threw pottery. One man burned beautiful designs into leather. I could have spent an entire day watching them.

"Why don't you and Paul get away for dinner?" Grandma asked, after we'd strolled through the shops.

"What will you and the girls have?"

"We'll find something. Don't worry."

Paul and I ate at the restaurant downstairs. It was a welcome break. When we returned to the room, no one was there. We looked out on the veranda and there they sat.

"What are you guys doing?" I asked.

"Watching Old Faithful."

We sat outside until the sun went down. The moon and stars took over the darkness. As we had traveled further west, the stars had become brighter and more plentiful. We had tried to look at the stars every night to find the different constellations. The Big Dipper was always easy and the first to become visible. The girls had learned how to find the Little Dipper and the North Star.

"There's the belt," Anne announced, pointing to the three consecutive stars that comprised Orion's belt.

I wished I had a book about the different constellations. Although we didn't know all the names and which stars belonged to which constellations, it was delightful to sit, necks stretched upward, under the flickering canopy.

We spent most of the next day in Yellowstone. We didn't want to leave. Our family feeling had returned with the charm of our surroundings. We had only 90 miles to go to the Grand Tetons.

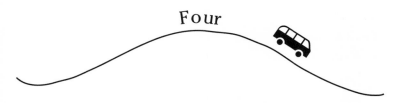

Four

Grandfather to the Rescue

When the going gets tough, listen to the
voices of experience.

It didn't take us long to realize that the wonderful family feeling was nothing more than an illusion. Anne and Clare began picking at each other within the first five miles as we drove towards the Tetons. After an hour, my nerves were as frayed as my husband's.

"We were too ambitious," I said to Paul. I couldn't tell if it was my lip or my right eyelid beginning to twitch.

"Yes, we were. The trip is too long."

"I'm not talking about the trip. I'm talking about them."

"What do you mean?"

"I mean we had three in a row. What were we thinking?"

"We weren't thinking. That was the problem." Paul smiled through HIS twitch, and patted my leg.

We heard a scream from the back. To describe it as bloodcurdling would not do it justice. It went right through my eardrums and hung there, convulsing. The little bones in my ears oscillated together so fast they didn't know what to do. The scream rang and resounded over and over again in my middle ear.

Paul pulled over.

I moved to the back even though it was the last place I wanted to be. We moved Anne to the front.

"She's turning around," Clare said. Clare's eyes had an eerie attraction for Anne's.

Anne turned, stuck out her tongue at Clare, and smiled. The magnetism went both ways.

Clare was gearing up for another primal shriek. My ears and twitches simply could not take it. I didn't want to lose it completely in front of my mother and yell SHUTUP at the top of my lungs. I had to act now.

"Don't even think about screaming again," I said. I had my arm around Erin. Her mouth was moving rapidly up and down in harmony with her clutched blanket.

I don't know why Clare stopped, but she did.

Nagging thoughts began crowding my mind until all I could think about was Home Sweet Home.

We stopped at a lake so we could stretch. I walked down to the water, as much to get away as to look for flat rocks for skipping. My "shadow" followed me and asked what I was doing.

"Look for the flat rocks, Erin," I said. "They're the best for skipping."

"Like this?" Erin held up a rock as big as her hand.

"More like this," I said, showing her my half-dollar sized rock. "Watch." I put the rock between my index finger and thumb. I snapped my wrist and the rock skipped three or four times.

Erin jumped up and down. She got busy looking for rocks for me.

Anne and Clare had been watching in a disinterested way. Now they both ran over.

"How'd you do that?" Anne asked. "Will you show me?"

"Sure."

"Show me, too," Clare said.

They got busy finding flat rocks. We worked on technique and snapping the wrist with the rock in our hand first. Then, we went down to the water to try it. I brought my arm to the side of my body and let the rock soar. It hit the surface perfectly and skipped eight times.

"Wow," Anne and Clare said together.

"I want to do that," Anne said.

"Me too," Clare said.

"Mom, I got a weal . . . weal . . . big . . . one." Erin paused with each word because the effort of lifting the real, real big rocks made her pant. She stood next to the water, heaved them with all her strength, and if they made it to the lake, they splashed. Then she did a little dance and went to find another.

I sat down on a log to watch and offer advice. Paul and Grandma had stayed by the van but now they came over to watch the excitement.

"Mom, are these good ones?" Anne showed me her rocks.

"They're fine. Remember to snap your wrist."

Clare threw one rock after another into the water. One of them skipped twice. She turned around to see if I was watching.

I was. I clapped for her. In no time, Anne was successful too, and we all clapped.

"I got a weal . . . big . . . wock," Erin squeaked. Her voice had gone into an octave that I wouldn't have believed was possible for the human ear to hear. I covered my ears and thanked God I wasn't a dog.

When we returned to the van, the talk was all about rock skipping.

"Mom, how'd you do that so many times?" Anne asked.

"I'd like to say I was just lucky, but I know it was skill." I rubbed my chest with my fist. In fact, it was my first time skipping eight times, but they didn't have to know that.

"How old were you when you learned?"

"I think I was six."

"Where'd you learn?" Clare asked.

"The Mississippi River. There was a beach by our house that we used to walk to."

"You're good at it," Clare said.

We arrived at our cabin on Colter Bay a half hour later. Erin took a nap and the rest of us read our books.

In the evening, we drove to a place that had hay wagons pulled by horses. All the way to the ranch, the talk in the car was about skipping rocks. What a simple thing that was to change the course of the conversation!

We stood waiting for our turn to get on the wagon. I thought we should go over to look at the horses in the corral.

"That's a boy horse, right?" Anne said. She pointed at a large stallion.

I didn't quite know what to say since there were a lot of people around. I didn't want to discuss male anatomy with my six-year-old so I didn't say anything. It was the coward's way out.

Anne wasn't going to let it go that easily. She looked back at the stallion. "All you have to do is look at their seat and you know if it's a boy," she announced.

Clare and Erin were becoming really interested in Anne's knowledge of boys.

"Let me see," Clare said.

"Me too," Erin said.

"Isn't that right, Dad?" Anne asked. "You just look at their seat."

"I guess so," Paul said. He moved them away from the corral. "Let's go wait for the wagon."

After an enjoyable ride in the hay wagon, we drove the short distance back to Colter Bay. The discussions in the van quickly soured as the disagreements between our two oldest turned ugly.

"Shutup, Clare," Anne snarled.

"She told me to shutup," Clare squealed.

"Anne, we don't talk like that." I gave our firstborn a pleading gaze.

The two of them were just getting revved up by the

time we parked next to the cabin. Paul, Grandma, and I emerged from the van, picked up Erin, and stepped inside. We hadn't said a word to Anne and Clare. They realized the audience was gone in a couple of minutes and rejoined the four of us.

Anne and Clare's lack of inhibition now carried over to the restaurants when we ate. Either Paul or I sat between them, trying to referee. The arbitrating didn't work, however, as they traded barbs across our worn-out torsos. The girl's hostility towards each other was present in our Scrabble and card games at night. There was no escaping.

That night we asked Grandma if she would like to fly home and we would pay for it. She could leave from Jackson Hole, Wyoming. The rest of us would have to forego the time we planned in Colorado and hightail it home. With two girls battling the whole 1200 miles, I was sure. It sounded dreadful but our options had narrowed.

"Mary Ann, do you want to fly home?" Paul asked Grandma.

"No, I'll stick it out," Grandma said.

"How would you feel about skipping Colorado?"

"Whatever you want."

"If you change your mind, let us know. We'll work it out."

"Thank you but I won't change my mind."

It was Sunday morning and Grandma wanted to go to church. We had read about an outdoor ecumenical service held every Sunday at 8:00 a.m. Grandma and I decided to go. We sat down on one of the folding chairs and faced the simple table serving as the altar. The temperature was about 60 degrees, and the air was crisp and clear. I filled my lungs to capacity.

The serrated peaks of the Tetons formed the forefront as we listened to the readings from Genesis. Not even a wisp of cloud interrupted the blue expanse above the mountains. The dark sapphire of the sky was a color I had never seen before. The words of the readings took on new meanings as we gazed at creation.

As we walked back to the van, we heard a man singing "How Great Thou Art." He had his arm around his son and his voice was as pure as our surroundings. It was truly a spiritual moment.

The adults in the family wanted to go into the town of Jackson Hole but we were afraid to get in the van with Anne and Clare. After vacillating for a while, we chose to brave the van ride. True to form, we had barely adjusted the mirrors when they started.

"She won't stop." Clare complained.

"Neither do you," I started to say. I was going to give a wonderful lecture on sisterly love when I was interrupted by a cacophony of loud noises from the back of the van. I kind of shrunk physically into the seat while my mental shrinking was downright embarrassing. I didn't confront them, tell them to stop, or tell them the consequences of their behavior. Instead of saying anything to either girl, I gave a sigh, and stared straight out the window.

As swollen with love as my heart had been the first

few days of the trip, it was now so constricted that it rattled around in my chest. With each cutting comment and each scream issuing forth from my daughters, my heart shriveled until it actually ached.

My thoughts took me to the upcoming evening journey to the laundromat. The more I thought about it, the more I looked forward to it. I'd bring a book and all I would hear was whirring machinery. It sounded peaceful and wonderful; I felt lucky that I got to do the laundry.

Anne and Clare wrangled for the half hour ride. Was it worth going anywhere? We were prisoners in the van while bickering sisters argued about everything including the weather.

We parked by the arch of antlers in Jackson Hole, and stumbled out of the van. Grandma and I put Anne, Clare, and Erin on a stagecoach for a ride around the town. Then we both collapsed on a bench. Neither of us said a word. Paul wandered away from us, arms clasped behind his back.

I couldn't figure out who Paul was talking to but it would change our lives forever. He leaned forward, intent on every word an elderly gentleman was saying. As the man spoke, Paul nodded his head in agreement.

I became more and more intrigued by what my husband was doing. He stood and shook the older man's hand vigorously.

Paul smiled as he came towards us. "I've got the answer," he said.

"To what?"

"To our problem in the car."

I was now very interested in what he was saying. I bent forward so I wouldn't miss a word.

"The guy I was talking to travels all over with his grandchildren. They've even gone as far as Alaska. He said fighting is never a problem."

"Never? I don't believe it."

"Listen. He said that at the beginning of each day he gives each one of them a roll of nickels. Every time they fight they get a nickel taken away."

"It really works?" I'd been an optimist all my life, but this was hard to believe.

"He said it does. But there's a trick. At the end of the day the kids can spend it any way they want. You can't say anything."

"It's worth trying," I said. "What do you think, Mom?"

"Sounds interesting," Grandma said.

The night before, Paul and I had agreed on one thing. We were never going to travel with our children again. I counted off 16 years of blissful summers while our neighbors hobbled home from their family vacations. By the time our girls were away at college, Paul and I could drive anywhere we wanted to, even to Alaska.

The only thing wrong with that image was that I liked to go places. I wanted to travel. I wanted the girls to experience the grandeur of mountains, the breadth of the country sky, the bracing smell in the air, the stars so plentiful that they illuminated the night. I wanted them to experience the peace that only nature can give. The city life couldn't compare when it came to quiet and serenity.

I had made up my mind. We would give the nickels a try as we headed towards Colorado. Some people might define this approach as akin to bribery. As I weighed the pros and cons, I remembered that we had been giving them small amounts of money in the evening for treats anyway. With this approach we would let them decide how much they had to spend each day. One thing was certain, so far the limp-wristed threats and rewards hadn't accomplished anything.

"Let's try it," I said.

The girls got off the stagecoach. We walked around in the town for a while but my mind was on one thing only—The Van Ride with our two older daughters.

As we got into the van, I felt almost carefree. Whatever they said to each other didn't matter because we had the countermove. Paul was smiling. We were ready for them.

"We're starting new rules for riding in the van," Paul began. "I'm going to explain them to you. We'll give you a roll of nickels at the beginning of each day."

"Ooh," Anne and Clare made the noise in tandem.

Paul had gotten their attention.

"Every time you poke, scream, yell, call names, or fight with each other we take away a nickel."

Anne and Clare made eye contact.

"She starts it," Clare said, pointing at Anne.

"I do not," Anne said.

"It doesn't matter who starts it. You don't have to react," I said.

"Let's get back to the rules so we all understand them," Paul said. "At the end of the day you can spend the money any way you want."

"Can I spend it on candy?" Erin piped up. She had a sweet tooth that could rival Winnie the Pooh's. I could well imagine our dental bills while her teeth rotted away.

"We won't say anything," Paul said.

Erin would probably have the entire two dollars to spend every evening. I kept my lips pressed together so I wouldn't comment on her soon-to-be decaying teeth. I had always been careful about how much candy the girls ate. In this case, I had to look at the whole picture. The mental health of the three adults took precedence over the dentist's bulging wallet, Mercedes, lake cabin, trip around the world . . .

"How about video games?" Anne asked.

"That's okay."

"Can I save it if I want?"

"Of course."

"Do I still get two dollars everyday even if I save some?" Anne asked. She wanted to understand the fine points before she committed herself.

"Every day is a brand new day," Paul said.

Clare had been quiet during the discussion.

"What do you think, Clare?" I asked.

"Anne always starts it."

"Don't react to her."

"I have to."

"Then you won't have many nickels left," I said.

"It's different when you don't start it," Clare persisted.

"So if Anne looks at you, she should get a nickel taken away, but if you scream and hit, you keep the nickel?"

"If she starts it."

"That's not the way it works, Clare," Paul said.

Five

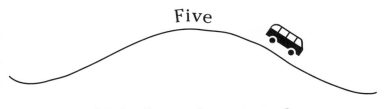

Skittles, Anyone?

To every set of actions are a set of consequences.

We had a rare silence on the way back to the cabin. The girls were mulling over what they valued most; tormenting each other or jingling nickels in their pockets as they decided what to spend them on. The stillness was fragile to say the least, so I didn't do my usual small talking.

I glanced in the rearview mirror. Anne was playing cards with Grandma. Clare was looking down at the floor. Erin had her blanket near her but she wasn't clasping it with jaws clenched. Paul was looking out the window.

We had an early dinner and then went back to the cabin.

There wasn't a lot of interest in Scrabble that night. Anne and Grandma had beaten me the night before and

49

they were still gloating about it. They called themselves "the champions," and gave the high-five to each other. I reminded them that it had been 24 hours since their upset and there were two of them. Of course, I didn't say one of them was a six-year-old.

Grandma described herself as "Just as happy if the other person wins" whenever a game was talked about. I heard her thanking Anne and saying, "I have lived for this; to beat your mother in Scrabble." The high-five again. I didn't know it was physically possible for mouths to smile so widely. I had always prided myself on being a gracious winner, saying, "I had all the good tiles," or "You opened up the board for me." There was no dealing with people who were poor winners, so I just laughed and let them have their moment.

I picked up the book I was reading and went outside. It was so pleasant. Soon Paul was out there too. Every so often Grandma or Anne or both of their grinning faces peeked out the door. They pointed at me and then looked at each other. "We beat her, Anne," Grandma would say. The high-five again.

When you travel with someone for two weeks straight, their true nature comes out.

Everyone was asleep by nine o'clock. We hoped to leave the Tetons by nine the next morning.

In the morning, we stopped for breakfast as soon as we found a restaurant.

After eating, we settled into our spots in the van. Paul

was in the driver's seat. In his hand were three rolls of nickels.

"I'm going to give each of you a roll of nickels," Paul said. He turned around and extended his arm toward the back. The girls each took a roll from his hand.

Paul had told me that the grandfather said the first few times you use the nickels the kids have to see them disappearing. After they get the idea, it doesn't matter if they actually have the roll of nickels in their hands.

"Good," Anne and Clare said. Their hands clasped the rolls. Erin didn't say anything. She put the roll under her blanket on her lap.

"Okay, let's go over this again," Paul said. "You have two dollars right now. "You'll have the same two dollars at the end of the day if you want to."

"I want to," Erin said.

"Good. Here are the rules. Anytime you fight physically or verbally with someone else, we take away a nickel."

"I won't fight," Erin said.

"What's verbally?" Clare asked.

"What you say."

"You mean we can't even talk?"

"I didn't say that. I said if you talk in a mean way you're going to lose a nickel."

"Even if I don't start it?" Clare asked.

I hoped in the future Clare could find a job where repetition and stubbornness were part of the job description.

"Even if you don't start it," I said. "It's up to you."

We didn't have to wait long for the nickels to start disappearing.

The discord started innocently enough with Anne teasing Clare about her shorts. I hadn't even remembered that they used to be Anne's.

"She's making fun of me."

"No, I'm not, you just think I am," Anne said.

Grandma was holding on to Erin. I looked at Paul and whispered, "This isn't going to work."

"The next comment by either one of you loses a nickel," Paul said.

But they were off and running.

"You did too make fun of me," Clare stated.

"I did not," Anne said. "You're so weird, Clare."

"Anne, give me a nickel," I said. It was shaping into another long day. She handed over the nickel without protest.

"She always makes fun of me," Clare stated. "She's a jerk."

"Clare, hand me a nickel," I said. Grandma was biting her lip as she snuggled with Erin.

"No, I won't. Because it's true."

"Now you lose two of them. Hand them over."

"I didn't dooo anything," Clare stated, with all the emphasis on the do word.

"Do you want it to be three?" I asked. I was getting exhausted already. This was not going to be so easy with our middle daughter. "Clare, if I have to crawl back there . . . ," I said leaving the rest of the sentence to her imagination. "Two nickels. Now."

Clare slowly opened the roll of nickels and handed me one nickel.

"I said two."

"It's not fair," she said as she gave me the second nickel.

"Life isn't," I said. "All I know is I'm going to be rich at the end of the day." Rich and twitching, I thought.

To say that was the end of the fighting would not be the truth. But by noon, I was seeing a light at the end of tunnel, at least with Anne. She didn't like surrendering her nickels.

We arrived at our hotel in Rawlings, Wyoming at five in the afternoon. Erin looked into the display of candy in the office with a little grin on her face. Her roll of nickels was still intact. She took some time deciding what she wanted. The man asked for a dollar.

"I have a whole dollar left," she chirped while holding her bag of candy.

"You can save it if you want," I said.

Anne had a dollar and 60 cents left of the original two dollars and Clare had 25 cents.

We carried our luggage to our two rooms and started to unwind. Erin ate her candy with her blanket around her shoulders. Every so often she looked in the bag to see how much was there. Anne had gone downstairs with Paul to check out the video games. I looked around for Clare and had no trouble figuring out what she was doing. She sat on one of the beds talking to Grandma. She had Grandma's full attention.

Clare could make her bright blue eyes as sad as a Basset Hound's. She summoned up all her abilities for the benefit of Grandma. Her eyes had never looked quite so sorrowful as they did at that moment.

About a half hour later, Grandma took me aside for a private talk.

"I probably shouldn't say anything but I have a suggestion," she began.

"I'm listening."

"Why don't you give up the nickel idea?"

"Has Clare been working on you?"

"No, I wouldn't say she's been working on me. But the poor thing only has a quarter."

Somehow, I didn't think of Clare as a "poor thing." There were times when I thought she belonged in Hollywood not St. Paul, Minnesota.

"So you don't think she did anything to deserve losing her nickels?" I asked.

"Some of the time."

I waited for the rest of it.

Grandma looked at me thoughtfully and said, "She's only four years old. I just don't like the whole thing. Some of her behavior hasn't been the best but much of it is normal four-year-old behavior."

"What should we do, then?"

"Ignore it. That's what I used to do."

"We tried ignoring it. We were all ready to scream." Not to mention that the various twitches on my face had each assumed their own rhythm. Thankfully, I wasn't a nervous person by nature or it could have been worse, much worse.

"It was pretty bad at times," Grandma agreed. She hesitated for a long couple of seconds. "I do have one more question," she said. "If you don't like it, just tell me."

"Okay."

"Can I give Clare another quarter? It wouldn't be from you or Paul and I'll make sure she knows that."

"Please don't. Clare may be only four years old, but she knows exactly what she's doing."

"Okay. I'll go along with whatever you and Paul say."

"Thanks, Mom."

Clare and Grandma conferred on the bed. Clare looked deep into Grandma's navy blue eyes. I'm sure she was picturing herself holding a big bag of candy while playing video games. Her hopes were dashed as she learned there would be no adding to her five nickels.

"Mom, would you take me downstairs to get some candy?" Clare asked quietly.

"Sure," I said.

When we came back to the room, Clare sat on the bed, opened her small bag of Skittles, and began to eat one Skittle at a time.

I knew if my eyes met Grandma's, she would be mouthing "poor thing" at me. So, with the sound of slow chewing in my ears, I looked out the window at the view of the parking lot.

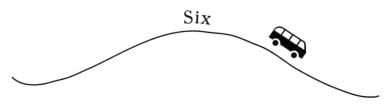

Six

Nickels From Heaven

A small price to pay for peace

The next morning I was as energetic as I had been when we left St. Paul. "Rise and shine," I said to Clare who was still sleeping. It was eight o'clock.

I had already showered, fixed my hair, put on my makeup, and had coffee with Grandma and Paul. Sometimes it bothered others but on vacation I could only be described as deliriously happy. I couldn't help it. The day awaited us.

As a last resort at home when the girls wouldn't get moving, I sang a repertoire of good morning songs to them. I usually started out with "Oh What a Beautiful Morning" from *Oklahoma*. If that didn't work, I moved on to "Good Morning, Good Morning, I'm So Glad to See You" from *Sesame Street*. If I had to sing more than one song, my alto voice became more like an opera diva. It never failed to roust them out of bed.

"Oh, what a beautiful . . . ," I sang in falsetto.

The covers were pulled back and Clare was up. It was hard to sing on an empty stomach so we were both spared further problems with ears and vocal cords.

We were driving by eight-thirty in the morning. The first thing we did, as always, was find a restaurant for breakfast. We found that it didn't make any sense to try for a late breakfast. The girls got squirmy and asked, "Are we stopping now?" every five minutes or so. Or one of them kept repeating, "I'm hungry." It took on a life of its own. I heard the words even when they weren't saying them.

By ten o'clock, we were pointed toward Colorado. The spiraling roads through the Rocky Mountains were difficult driving. Luckily, we didn't hear the high-pitched screeches of earlier days. We could concentrate on keeping the van in the middle of the slender lanes without facial muscles spasming. We curved around a precipitous bend when I noticed three plain white crosses next to the edge.

"I wonder what those crosses are for?"

"I don't know if I should tell you," Paul said.

"Why? Tell me."

"It's places that people have gone over the edge."

"In their car?"

"Car and all."

"Do the crosses mean they died?"

Paul nodded his head.

I was glad he was driving at that moment. My heart kind of slackened in my chest thinking of those poor people. Twelve thousand feet was a long way from the ground.

I had decided with all our mountain driving that sealevel had more than a few advantages. The driving was easy when the streets faced each other in perfect right angles. The drivers were relaxed as they waved to each other at stop signs.

Another advantage was that the oxygen was dense. A deep breath, saturated with molecules, went into the bloodstream and traveled all over the body. The brain had millions of molecules to choose from. Maybe this was the biggest advantage. I liked my brain getting oodles of oxygen. It worked better. At these high altitudes, the brain couldn't afford to pass up even a single molecule. I hadn't had any problems with the thin air so far, but now my breathing was becoming more and more rapid.

I stared straight ahead on the curvy cross-laden road and didn't utter a sound. With my fingernails in my mouth awaiting a bite, the words would have sounded more like blubbering than speaking and I didn't want to scare the girls.

We arrived in Rocky Mountain National Park well before five o'clock in the afternoon. The hotel had a swimming pool, the first since Rapid City. None of us wanted to budge for the rest of the day.

It truly was fate the day Paul met the traveling grandfather in Jackson Hole. Since two of the three adults were on the verge of losing it completely, we needed direction from someone. What are the chances of meeting one person who would change your outlook on everything from bribery to promoting dental caries?

After the first trying day, the grandfather's nickels worked like a wonderful magic spell on Anne and Clare. I won't say that there were no altercations between them, but Anne became too busy playing cards and reading to think about what Clare was doing or wearing. At a certain point—I'm not sure when—Clare decided it wasn't worth it to keep looking for things she could react to, and she went back to her books. Erin took a two hour nap without being jolted out of dreams of unlimited candy and treats.

By the end of the first day in Colorado, Clare's and Anne's senses of humor were coming back. I was heartened by this return of humor because Clare was one of those people who was naturally funny. When she wasn't protesting social injustice in the family, she was clever and witty. Anne had a drier sense of humor than Clare but it was just as funny. And when Anne laughed, she still belly laughed like a baby.

I had also missed their nicknames. Annie had become Anne Rachel and Clare Bear had become Clare Elizabeth in the preceding days of war.

The girls were happy with how much of the two dollars they had left after the drive into Colorado. Erin had the full two dollars, Anne had one dollar and 90 cents, and Clare had one dollar and 60 cents. The three girls each had a bag of candy to hang onto. They brought them down to the pool and the indoor hot tub.

"Would you watch my candy?" Clare asked me.

"Sure, Bear." Things were looking up.

"Mine too?"

"Sure, Annie," Things were really looking up.

They got into the hot tub together. Things couldn't have gotten much higher.

The next day we went to the town of Estes Park. The girls had slept late so we waited until after lunch. With the mountains all around, the town lay in a beautiful setting.

It was Paul's birthday and we wanted to celebrate. Everyone had the job of keeping him occupied while the others shopped. My mother and I bought a cake and some candles. I found an assortment of different combs including a mustache comb. The girls each got him a little present. They were so excited about the cake, they couldn't wait.

"Do you think Dad will like the cake?"

"I think so."

"Do you think he'll like his presents?"

"I think so."

"Do you think he'll use the mustache comb?"

"I think so. I hope so."

We went to dinner at five o'clock, went back to the

motel, lit the candles, sang "Happy Birthday" many times, cut the cake, and opened the presents.

Paul combed his mustache with the little comb.

It was a wonderful celebration.

I even sang Irish songs before the girls went to sleep. As much as they disliked my singing in the morning, they asked me to sing to them at night. My voice was limited in range but I loved the Irish songs. I sang "The Rose of Tralee," "Too Ra Loo Ra Loo Ra," and the last was my favorite "Danny Boy." The girls didn't mind that I had trouble hitting all the notes.

I'm sure the man in the Old Faithful Inn would have sung them much better, but then he wouldn't have been laying in bed with three girls hugging him.

I was a little worried about the long drive through Nebraska and Iowa. Would the nickels continue their enchantment with the hours of driving ahead?

We started early the next morning, deciding we would drive until we had all had enough.

We bought some sandwiches and had a picnic in a pretty park in the northern part of Nebraska. We pointed to Lincoln, Nebraska on the map as a good place to stop. But when we got close to Lincoln, we drove on, making it as far as Grand Island, Nebraska before we quit for the night.

Each of the three girls had two full dollars left when we found our motel. They picked out their treats, put on their swimming suits, and went down to the pool.

I wished that I could have thanked the wise grandfather. As far as I was concerned he and his nickels had come directly from heaven.

The next day we were on the road early again. We stopped at Offnut Air Force Base in Omaha, the site of the Strategic Air Command. The hour-long look around the museum provided an interesting break from driving. Later we stood outside next to the B-52s.

"Wow, these are big," Clare said.

"Like Tyrannosaurus Rex," Anne said.

Erin leaned against Paul at the mention of Tyrannosaurus Rex.

We returned to the van and headed towards Iowa.

Iowa was lush and green with mile after mile of perfect rows of corn. The stalks swayed together with the warm breezes. We thought we would stop in Des Moines for the night, but the vote was six to zero to keep driving until we got home.

The most unusual thing happened when we crossed the Minnesota border with Iowa. The sun was on its downward curve towards the horizon.

"A rainbow. A rainbow," Anne exclaimed.

We looked out the windows and saw the most brilliantly colored rainbow. The colors were so crisp that it looked as if there was a line between each of them. The perfect arch gave the illusion that we were driving right under it. We could see it on either side. Soon our exclamations became even louder.

"There's another one," Clare cried out, pointing to the sky.

"Let me see." Anne smashed her face against the window.

"Let me see." Erin's nose was completely flattened on the glass windowpane.

"Oh, my gosh. Look at that," Paul said.

Next to the first rainbow was a twin. Not quite as brilliant as the first, but nonetheless, a full arch. So we drove along, loving our Minnesota with a double archway as a welcome.

"I have never seen anything like that," Grandma said.

"Me either," I said.

"It's beautiful. Absolutely gorgeous."

I was glad I wasn't driving because I couldn't keep my eyes off the sight on either side of us. The rainbows were still escorting us as the sky gave way to twilight. We strained to see the colors. Red became just a blush and the green faded into the trees. Soon the darkness wrapped around us and the colors were gone.

"That was the best rainbow," Anne said.

"Rainbows," said Clare. "There were two."

"The best rainbows."

"I love twin rainbows the best," Erin said.

We walked into our house with the moon and stars shining. We had the whole winter ahead of us to discuss the next summer's travels. The Grand Canyon would be a great place to visit.

With our nickels we could go anywhere.

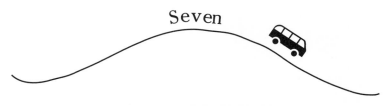

Seven

The Right Formula

*Each new person changes family
dynamics forever and ever.*

Winter was not the quiet time we had envisioned. Anne began first grade, we sold our house, I found out I was pregnant again, we moved on January second, we painted walls, and removed old carpeting while I got fatter and fatter. Our fourth daughter was born on June 1,1986.

Instead of driving to the Grand Canyon or elsewhere, the entire summer was spent taking care of baby Colleen. She was a cheerful, calm baby which was lucky for her and all of us.

Anne picked her up immediately whenever she made a peep. Three very willing sisters provided bottles, gave baths, ran to get diapers, put powder on, changed sleepers, and carried the diaper bag.

Our days were filled with meeting the baby's needs. She had four faces staring at her whenever she drank a bottle; four faces staring at her whenever she had a bath. She was kissed so many times in one day that I told the girls to move their kisses around so she wouldn't get indentations in her head.

I had breast fed the other three while they were getting up at night. I tried to do the same with Colleen, but I was so tired after spending just a day and a half in the hospital that it wasn't going very well. I didn't have enough milk. After a week, I gave up and decided to use the formula alone.

The squabbles started before I was fully recovered.

"It's my turn to feed the baby," Clare said.

Anne ignored her and continued feeding three-week old Colleen her bottle.

"Mom, she did it last time," Clare shouted.

"Clare, stop yelling. Is that true, Anne?" I asked.

"I guess so."

"You have to let the other girls have time with Colleen, too."

"I never get to feed the baby," Erin twittered.

"I don't either," Clare said.

I was thinking I didn't either, but it really didn't matter. This was coming to a head quickly. I was beginning to feel like I was in the van again with brawling sisters. The problem was mainly Anne and Clare, but Erin was putting in her two-cents worth, too. She had become more assertive in the last year with her two older sisters. Although I felt that was good for Erin, at this point I didn't need three girls fighting. Since they all wanted the baby to themselves, it was no holds barred.

At least two girls quarreled at all times. Sometimes I could have sworn I had a dozen girls in the house. The only thing that stopped their incessant arguing was the rare occasion when the baby started crying because of their noise. The voices lowered but whoever had been fighting blamed the baby's crying on their sparring partner. It was always the other guy's fault. I was so exhausted by the time Paul got home every day, I wanted to go right to bed. There I could rip out my hair in peace and quiet.

Nickels wouldn't work in this situation, but I thought I better address the problems. Otherwise, they'd be fighting all summer over the baby. The poor baby was going to wish she was somewhere else. I had to deal with the immediate situation, then I could try a more long-term solution.

"Clare, you can feed her the next bottle, okay?"

"Okay, but I never get to hold her either."

"That's a different issue. Let's take care of the bottles first. Erin, after Clare, it's your turn."

"Okay," Erin said.

We had already divided her body into four different sections for her baths. The baths took a full hour. As long as someone was spraying Colleen with the water, she stayed warm. I took the head and bottom. The three girls had their own leg front and back, or both arms. The chest and stomach was also separated. If one of the other girls went out of their territory with soap and washcloth, the area was washed over again. One of them remarked that we should just have the baby marked with magic marker so there wouldn't be any mistakes. The three agreed.

"I think Dad and I are going to wash the baby after you're all in bed."

"No," the three said in harmony.

"No magic markers, then."

No one ever brought it up again. Colleen continued to laugh as we soaped, sprayed, and powdered her.

Now I had to think about how I was going to divide the bottle feeding. The mornings posed the biggest problem. Paul took the early morning feeding, then went to work before the three older girls woke up. Colleen was back in bed by six-thirty. Her three big sisters were usually awake by seven or seven-thirty. They waited for Colleen to wake up so they could give her her bottle. When she stirred about nine o'clock, my face and three other faces peered into her crib.

The three sisters were blessed with plenty of young vigor while I dragged my body to the kitchen to warm up the bottle. Anne usually carried Colleen downstairs and then announced it was her turn to feed the baby.

"No, it's not, it's my turn," Clare said. "Mom," she yelled.

"I never get a turn," Erin said while holding her blanket. She liked to cover Colleen with her blanket while she fed her.

I was glad they were so interested in Colleen but I was getting exasperated. I thought about telling them I was going to take over all of the feedings. Then a brilliant idea came to me.

"This is what we're going to do," I began.

"About what?" Anne asked.

"About the baby."

"What's wrong with the baby?"

"Nothing's wrong. Let me finish."

All eyes and hopefully ears were glued on me. "You all want to give the baby her bottles, right?"

"Right." The three agreed.

"Every third morning will be your morning."

"I don't get it," Clare said.

"Well. Today is your morning, Clare. That means you feed Colleen her bottle and she's yours until she takes a nap."

"You mean I can hold her without someone else grabbing her?"

"That's what I mean."

"Cool," Clare said.

Clare fed Colleen her bottle, burped her, and wiped her mouth. I put the baby on the inside of the couch so she could lie with Clare. Every 30 seconds or so, Colleen got another kiss. In an hour, I took Colleen and put her back in the crib for a nap.

The next day was Erin's turn. I helped her with the bottle and burping. Then, I put Colleen on the inside of the couch again and she was all Erin's.

This worked so well that we continued with it throughout the summer. I didn't have to keep track of whose turn it was; the girls did that just fine.

Every morning the four of us walked with baby Colleen in the stroller. The girls took turns pushing her and answering questions from the neighbors. In the afternoons, the girls were busy with friends or doing other things. I loved the afternoons because I had some quiet time with my brand new daughter.

September came quickly. Anne started second grade and Clare started kindergarten. This was nice for Erin, who was more reticent than the other two. She had about three hours every day alone with the baby and me. To Erin's delight, she got to feed Colleen all her bottles when the others were at school.

We didn't drive to the Grand Canyon the next summer either. Instead, we left one-year-old Colleen with grandparents and took our three older girls to Wisconsin Dells. It wasn't the same without her.

"I wonder what Colleen is doing."

This statement was made many times a day by one of us.

"Do you think she'll forget us?"

The girls worried about this possibility, especially on day three. I assured them that this wouldn't happen; that she remembered us.

"Do you think she's mad at us for leaving her?" Anne asked.

"No."

One night we saw the Tommy Bartlett show. Water-skiers thrilled us with many amazing tricks in their fast-moving performance. I loved it except something was missing.

"Colleen would have loved Tommy Bartlett," Clare said.

That's what was missing!

We took a ride on the Wisconsin Ducks, which are amphibious watercraft from World War Two. We had a hair-raising ride through the woods and ended up in Lake Delton. The driver had to engage many gears to make the transition from land to water.

"The Ducks," Erin began, "Colleen would've loved them."

We took a trip down the beautiful Wisconsin River to see the unusual rock formations. We went miniature golf-ing, saw the Indian ceremonial, and spent a day at a water park.

"There were places for Colleen to play in the water park. Somebody would've stayed with her. Let's never leave her again," Anne declared.

All heads nodded in agreement.

We left early the fourth day. The talk all the way home was who was going to pick Colleen up first.

I really thought it should be me but Paul settled it with a few words. "I'm picking her up first. No arguments."

Now the choice was who was going to be second,

third, etc. I had the suspicion that I would be bringing up the rear.

I'll never forget the look on Colleen's face when the five of us came walking in the door. It was absolute delight.

True to our word, we never traveled without our youngest again.

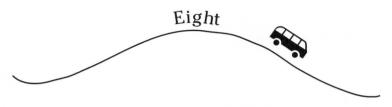

Eight

On The Road Again

With children, the spirit of adventure brings
the most unexpected results.

The summer of 1990, Colleen turned four years old, and we were back on the road again.

It had been a hotter than usual summer in Minnesota.

Paul had four vacation days in August. We decided to drive north to Lake Superior and into Canada. It was rarely hot there and the scenery was spectacular.

The nickels were out again. The three girls explained to Colleen the rules for driving in the van. She listened seriously and said, "I'll have two dollars every day."

Colleen had been wearing eyeglasses for about three months. Her eyes turned into the corners, especially when she looked to the side. The glasses were supposed to help straighten her eyes and, hopefully, avoid surgery.

The strong magnification made her black eyes huge behind the lenses. We all told her how beautiful she looked.

Toby's, in Hinckley, was our first stop. As we ate, we talked about all the places we were going to see. Paul and I had been to Northern Minnesota several times but the girls had only been as far as Duluth. We finished breakfast and continued heading north with a dozen donuts for the next morning. The four girls protested as we drove through Duluth without stopping. They loved the city; watching the huge ore ships come into the harbor was a favorite thing to do. We promised them that we would stop on our way home.

We pulled the van over when we saw the sign for Gooseberry Falls. I remembered seeing it for the first time when I was a little girl. To see the Lower Falls, we had to walk down never-ending stairs. I hadn't thought about the number of steps when I was younger. I did now. There's nothing like age to promote attention to details.

The girls ran ahead of Paul and me. We warily negotiated the steep steps while trying to look ahead to where our children were. By the time Paul and I reached the bottom of the stairs, the girls were skipping along on the slippery rocks with Colleen in tow. They wanted to be closer to the wonderful waterfall. I pictured my youngest being dropped on one of the rocks, never to be the same again. Even though I had no desire to be almost underneath the waterfall, I had to follow them to assure her safety. With that thought in mind, I went ahead of Paul who was readying the camera.

I found it slow going on the smooth wet rocks. I wished with each step that I had suction cups on the bottom of my tennis shoes. I was so engrossed in trying to find the flattest stones to walk on that I lost sight of our children. I looked up and spotted the four of them together. At least, I was heading in the right direction. I reached them short of breath and thinking about how I was going to get back to Paul, the stairs, and the van.

"Hi, girls."

"Hi, Mom."

"I'll help Colleen," I said emphatically. I took in another deep breath as I steadied myself on the perfect-sized boulder. I reached out my hand and felt the boulder shift. I pulled my hand back until I found my footing again.

"She's fine," Anne stated. "In fact, we're all ready to go back."

"Really. Don't you want to look any longer?"

"No, we looked at it."

"Isn't it beautiful?"

There was a whoosh of air as they scurried past me, feet barely touching stone.

I pivoted each of my feet separately, as I turned my body around. I was glad Colleen wasn't with me at this point. I tried to follow the girl's lead but their footsteps had already disappeared on the wet rocks.

Heartened to see a large, flat slab in front of me, I

decided to blaze my own trail. I stretched my right foot, ankle, calf, thigh in the air, searching for the rock. My toes, then the sole, then the heel of my right foot found the rock. My left leg elongated, until I did something that resembled the splits. Even in my earlier athletic days, I had never been able to do the splits. This was the best near-splits I had ever done. I would have been excited under different circumstances but I didn't want to be stuck in such a compromising position for long. I had to take action. I hauled my left leg over with the help of my left arm. With both feet planted on the rock, I peered off to the right, left, and straight ahead. There was no place to step. Everything was submerged.

I was stranded.

I searched for anyone who looked familiar. I wasn't ready to yell HELP yet and make a total fool out of myself. Panic began to gnaw at me. It wasn't a bad panic because the worst thing that could happen would be that I would slip on a submerged stone, get both my tennis shoes filled with icy water, have my feet fly up in the air, and bash my head against my perfect flat perch. Never to be the same again.

"Mom, go this way," Anne shouted. She pointed to a rock I hadn't seen.

After the gracefulness of getting onto this rock, getting off it should have been a piece of cake. If only there were some hand rails. My arms automatically went up at a right angle to my body for balance. I felt like a tightrope walker.

My toes went to the edge of the rock that Anne stood upon. She grabbed my arm and pulled me onto the rock. Anne led me to the safety of Paul and the other girls.

"I'm glad you went to save Colleen," Paul said, smiling.

"She would have been in big trouble without me," I said as I laughed.

"I got some good pictures."

"You did?"

"I did."

I thanked God for limber, almost twelve-year-olds for the sake of both my body and our family photo albums.

We still wanted to see Split Rock Lighthouse before we stopped in Lutsen for the night. We drove along the highway when I saw a petting zoo I remembered from many years before. I should have noticed that there were no cars in the parking lot. We had to go through the gift shop to get to the animal area. We bought some corn kernels to feed them.

The woman opened the door to let us out into the yard. The six of us had our cones with the corn inside. The animals came to greet us, mouths agape. We were crowded in the entrance with the door closed behind us. We were the only human beings there.

It was different than it had been when I was young. The animals were much bigger!

Anne didn't like the 150 pound young buck with sprouting antlers. He squeezed against her, trying to steal her cone. She threw it up in the air and the buck disappeared.

The llamas were not to be outdone. They came over to us looking for food.

I had Colleen with me and Paul was moving the other girls into the yard. For some reason these animals didn't bother me at all. Thinking about being crushed by large animal bodies, or gored by fur-covered antlers, didn't disturb me in the same way as dashing my head against a stone.

"Move out of the way," I said to the pair of 100 pound llamas.

We walked into the yard. I held Colleen's hand, wanting her to see the porcupines and raccoons. To tell you the truth, I found it odd that porcupines were in a petting zoo. But then, bucks with antlers weren't the usual fare either.

The girls petted some cute little goats. Our food disappeared quickly. Some of the animals were much less interested in us now that we were empty-handed. Anne was happy with this development, but the young buck had taken a fancy to her. Anne came to stand beside me. The buck stood beside her.

"I want to go," Anne said.

"Okay, let's go."

We made it back to the door without calamity, when the buck made an abrupt move and blocked our way out. Anne was starting to hyperventilate.

"Move," I yelled. I hoped the woman inside would hear me, but there was no response.

The buck stayed put as he ogled Anne. It was hard

to tell if he was blinking, or just trying to show off his sweeping eyelashes.

Paul came over, and we both shouted MOVE at the same time.

The buck must have decided Anne wasn't his type after all because he gave us room to open the door. We were through the door and out in the car in a couple of seconds. No one wanted to search for trinkets in the gift shop.

Split Rock Lighthouse was a few short miles from Gooseberry Falls. Anne remained quiet en route. The lighthouse—as interesting as I remembered it—was completed in 1910 and used until 1960. Since then, it's been part of the Minnesota State Park system.

We toured the lighthouse and walked up the steps to see the huge refractory lens. The octagonal lighthouse stood high above Lake Superior with a dazzling view of the Lake. We inspected the lighthouse keeper's house, looked at the other buildings, and took some pictures with the Lake in the background.

We meandered to the gift shop area.

Anne's vivaciousness hadn't returned. I could have teased her, but I waited for her to bring it up.

"Why do you think he liked me?"

"I don't know. Maybe you look like a deer."

"No, I mean it. Why did he like me?"

"Maybe you smell good."

"I don't have any perfume on." Anne put her fingers in

her mouth and began to chew her nails. She hadn't done that since the bear park in Rapid City.

"They have better senses of smell than we do."

"Maybe he's really dumb," ten-year-old Clare interjected.

"Maybe," I agreed.

"I'm glad he wasn't full grown," Anne said with a shudder.

Colleen and Erin came over to hear what we were talking about. I pushed up Colleen's glasses on her small nose. One of us did this many times a day.

"You guys ready to go?" I asked.

"Yup."

We arrived in the Lutsen area in time for an early dinner. Each of the girls had two dollars of nickels left. They had had some minor disagreements in the van, but nothing that warranted a nickel being taken away.

We finished eating and went outside to sit and marvel at my favorite lake.

Whenever I've been to what Minnesotans call the North Shore, I am astounded by the beauty. The waterfalls and rushing streams all flow down to magnificent Lake Superior. I roll down the windows in the car to hear the surging water, and to smell the sweet air. Rolling hills and picturesque forests make every turn something that could be on a postcard. All I can do is gaze in wonder.

People compare Lake Superior to the ocean. The wildness and power are there when a strong wind blows.

When the wind is elsewhere, the gentle lapping of the water gives me a quiet, peaceful soul.

And the stars. What can I say about the stars?

We were on our way to Thunder Bay, Canada, by nine the next morning. We ate breakfast in Grand Marais, another of my favorite spots.

We drove by Grand Portage because we were planning to tour Old Fort William in Canada. The voyageurs had used both places for their fur trading.

The sun shining on the water made the lake shimmer like crystalline jewels as far as I could see. As the altitude climbed above sea-level, scenic overlooks began to appear. One of the overlooks before the passage into Canada was so gorgeous that I was left open mouthed; not unlike our friendly buck in the petting zoo.

The sign saying "Welcome to Canada" greeted us. We consulted our map and then headed in the direction of Old Fort William. The temperature climbed with the altitude. Hot waves rose from the asphalt as we drove away from the cool lake breezes.

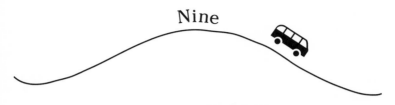

Nine

Paper Suits Me

*Besides love, the greatest gift you can give your
children is laughter, especially at yourself.*

It must have been the heat.

Ninety-five degrees and humid gets to me; not only
physically, but mentally as well.

We had traipsed around Old Fort William, wowing
over beaver pelts while the sweat ran down our six faces,
upper torsos, and settled in our belly buttons. It was
hard to walk by the time we got to the encampments behind the fort. Since none of our four children said, "Who
cares," I had to feign an interest in the guide and his
story. Wrung out is a nice way of putting how I felt by the
end of the tour.

Paul had booked a hotel in Thunder Bay that had
a giant waterslide in the pool area. Our children didn't

know about it yet. As we drove towards the hotel, I thought all I would want to do was take a shower, change clothes, and sit watching my husband and children propelling themselves down the slide.

The girls screamed when they saw it. They put on their swimming suits, walked around the whole pool area, and counted the ten twists and turns of the slide. Then they jumped into the water and waited for the slide to open. I sat happily at a table with Colleen on my lap.

The slide opened at precisely five o'clock.

"Can Colleen go down with me?" Anne asked.

"How can she?"

"On my lap. I'll hang on to her."

"Are you sure?" I asked. Colleen had been in the water from the time she was a baby and she was already a fair swimmer. She didn't mind getting her face or anything else wet. But she hadn't gone down a waterslide before. From the time Paul made the reservations, I had planned on her being with him.

"I'm sure."

"What do you think, Paul?" I asked.

"I think it's okay. Anne's careful."

"Guard her with your life," I said to Anne.

"I will."

I took Colleen's glasses off and put them on the table. I blew up her swimmies, the inflatable arm bands that went on her upper arms. She was ready. Anne took her hand as they headed for the stairs. Clare and Erin followed right behind them. Paul waited in the pool at the end of the slide.

I don't remember if our children were the first ones down the slide, but once they started coming, it was one after the other. They seemed to be going so fast.

"Be careful," I yelled.

Anne and Colleen had just finished the slide. Anne landed standing up as she lifted her sister into the air. Since there was no splash, not even a drop of water fell onto Colleen's hair.

Colleen climbed up the ladder on the edge of the pool and stood in front of me. Her feet alternated her weight as she shifted back and forth, black eyes glistening.

"Was it fun?"

"Really fun. Can I go again?"

"Sure," I said.

I was beginning to wish that I hadn't forgotten my swimming suit. Every single person got right back in line. It just looked like so much fun. Like Colleen, I had never gone down a waterslide before. But unlike the rest of my family, I was afraid of the water. It was too bad they didn't make swimmies big enough to fit around my motherly upper arms.

"Why didn't I bring my swimming suit?" I asked my husband.

"Are you thinking about going down the slide?"

"Maybe."

"Really? I can't believe it." Paul had already gone down the slide several times.

"I'm thinking about it, but I can't go down in my under-wear." The thought of years of cellulite build-up and sag-ging flesh was not a pretty thought, and it would be an even less pretty sight. "I wish I had my suit," I said.

"Go to the front desk and ask if they sell any," Paul said.

"Do you think they do?"

"I don't know. Ask."

I mulled it over for a short while. I couldn't wonder any longer. I walked out of the pool area and approached the front desk.

"Ma'am, um, this might sound like a weird question, but do you sell swimming suits?"

"Sure do. They're ten dollars," the woman behind the desk said.

"Great." I couldn't believe my luck.

"One piece or two, Hon?" the woman asked.

"Can I look at both of them?"

"Sure." She held up the print two-piece bikini.

"Isn't that kind of small?" I asked. It looked as if there was barely enough material to cover my well endowed hind end. Anyway, my bikini days had gone by the way-side after four pregnancies, stretch marks, and perma-nent weight gain.

"Wanna look at the one piece?" She held up the one-piece suit. It was the same flowery design as the bikini.

"Okay. What material are they made of?"

People were gathered behind me at the desk. Some of them were listening to my conversation and looking at each other.

"Paper," she said.

"Paper!" The image I had of myself catapulting down the slide as my suit disintegrated was frightening to say the least. "That's okay. Thanks anyway." I started walking away from the desk.

"They're very strong, miss."

"Strong enough for a waterslide?"

"Yes. Look." She took the suit and pulled at the seams. The stitches didn't budge.

"Do they rip at all?" I examined the one-piece. I stretched the seams in all different directions. There were no gaps in the tight sutures.

"Never had a problem," the woman said.

People were catching each other's eyes, mouthing "Sure" and "I want to see this."

"Okay." I handed her a ten dollar bill.

"Thank you, miss. I hope you enjoy the slide."

"I hope so too. Thank you." It came out in a sincere way when I said it, but I wondered if I should be so polite as I prepared to make a total fool out of myself.

"This heat is something, eh? It's never this hot," the woman said almost apologetically.

Now I felt more at home. The Canadians talked as much about the weather as Minnesotans.

I went back to the room and changed into my paper

suit, inspecting the texture again. It seemed strong, more like heavy linen than paper. Just in case of a rupture, though, I wore a tee shirt over it.

"I'm ready," I said when I arrived at the pool.

My family was waiting to escort me to the steps going up to the waterslide. There were two girls in front of me and two others holding up the rear. Paul was in the pool anticipating my landing.

"How do you slow down?" I kept asking.

No one answered. My children glanced at each other. The eye contact with me was non-existent.

"C'mon, Mom," Anne said. She walked in front of me with Colleen.

We made it up the probably 50 steps without mishap. I didn't realize it was so high until I got to the top.

The line moved rapidly. Anne and Colleen departed.

It was my turn now. No one was in front of me. The pounding in my chest let me know my heart was still beating. The blood coursed fiercely through my body. I was quickly going into the "fight or flight" mode.

"Do I sit?"

The lifeguard at the top of the slide nodded his head.

I sat waiting for my signal to go. I swallowed the modest amount of saliva left in my mouth.

"How do you slow down?" I asked.

He looked at me strangely and said, "Just sit up straight."

"Okay," I was sitting up straighter already.

"Go." The man motioned to me.

"ME! Right now?"

I was starting to sweat but it wasn't from the heat. I stared at the long line behind me. I decided it would be more embarrassing crawling over strangers and family than drowning in the three and a half feet of water at the end.

"Lady, you can go."

I heard the words as I gingerly pushed myself down the slide. I thought I heard a rusty hinge creaking. I hoped it wasn't the slide. I bent forward slightly. I quickly corrected myself by sitting up like a straight-back chair.

Creak. Creak. Creeeak.

Good, it's just my waist, I thought.

I approached the first curve. I realized astutely that I had no control in the curves at all. I thought about swearing, and then, luckily, thought again. I knew the s-h word would echo and reverberate throughout the slide. My children, especially four-year-old Colleen, would probably be traumatized for life.

I was going too fast.

Maybe if I put my legs up along the sides more, I'd slow down.

I did seem to slow down a fraction of a second but I knew I had to concentrate the entire length of the slide. The man had told me not to put my hands on the sides. I tried to keep them on my thighs although I needed them for balance.

The bottom of my paper suit seemed to be filling with water but I didn't dare try to get it out. I pictured myself careening to the top of a curve, hanging suspended for a split second, and landing on my side. Or worse, I could flip over and land on my face with water rushing up my nose.

Don't worry about the water, I told myself as my buttocks swung from side to side.

I weighed more with each passing second.

Paul said he would be waiting at the end for me. I hoped he planned to catch me and keep me from going under water. I went around the S shaped curve and saw the opening that signaled the end of the slide. I wanted to land without so much as a ripple, like Anne and Colleen had. I saw Paul standing in the water. That was my last conscious thought before my body flew through the air. I hit the surface, water-filled buttocks first, with a large splatter as my face and every other part of me went completely under. I was still trying to stand when Paul grabbed my arm and pulled me up.

"Are you okay?" he said. There was a mixture of laughter and clapping around the pool.

"I'm okay. I can't believe how fast it is. I felt like a rocket on that last curve." I stated this fact loudly so everyone could hear.

"Mom, are you going again?" little Colleen asked.

There are some experiences in life that truly are "Once is not enough." How could I say no to a four-year-old when she was almost jumping up and down?

"I think I'll go again," I said. I went back to the steps and had one of my daughters shield me while I let out the ten pounds of water collected at the bottom of my suit. First the one side, then the other. I felt lighter already.

We climbed the stairs quickly, it seemed, and soon I was at the top awaiting my turn.

When the pool man saw me, he was too polite to let out a groan. I didn't ask how to slow down because I already had that information. And when he said, "Go," I went. The third time I actually landed feet first, toes touching the bottom of the pool.

There was more applause from the bystanders. I took a creaky bow.

After my tenth slide down, I decided to quit. The paper suit was miraculously intact.

Paul told me all the people around the pool agreed that they had never seen a person go down a waterslide so slowly!

The girls continued gliding down the slide until ten o'clock when it closed. Colleen went alone by the end of the evening with Anne waiting at the end to catch her. As before, not a drop of water touched Colleen's hair.

We went back to our room to dry off and put on our pajamas.

They laughed about me going down the waterslide saying that my mouth was a perfect O when I splatted into the water. I don't know why I thought Paul could catch me; I wasn't a featherweight like my youngest daughter. I probably would have knocked him backwards as I touched down feet first into his chest.

"I can't wait to go down a waterslide again," I said.

"I hope the picture turns out, Dad," Clare said.

Everyone looked at Paul.

"Picture, what picture?" I asked.

"The picture Dad took when you came out of the slide," Anne said. "I can't wait to see it."

"No wonder I went completely under," I said. "I didn't know you were taking my picture." How many more surprises were in store for me?

"I had to. It was the funniest thing I've ever seen," Paul said. He looked a little sheepish.

How quickly they turn on you.

All eyes were on me. Erin and Colleen were almost beside themselves trying not to laugh. I realized that I could give my girls a lesson in good sportsmanship. Posterity would see me, their ancestor, soaring through the air, arms and legs splayed, in a paper suit, my mouth forming a perfect O. It was pretty funny.

I started laughing. "Was my mouth really a perfect O."

"It was perfect," Paul said.

The six of us laughed. Secretly I hoped the picture wouldn't turn out.

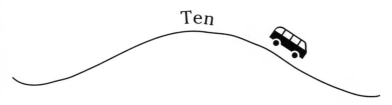

Ten

Life in the Slow Lane

In the slow lane,
it's the finish that counts.

I would have liked to go all the way around Lake Superior but we didn't have enough time. And I liked the Canadians; they were friendly and helpful. One of the Canadians I had talked to said if we got the chance we should go to Kakabeka Falls.

It was a little bit out of our way, but we drove to the wide, rocky waterfall on our way back to Minnesota the next morning. We heard the turbulent water long before it came into our sight.

"This is impressive," I said.

"Yes, it is," Paul said.

A bridge spanned the Falls. We stood on it and gazed

miles into the distance. Far ahead we could see the river zigzagging through the thick forest.

"Do you like it, Erin?" I asked.

"Mm, hmm."

"I do too. It's beautiful. I love it."

"Why don't you marry it then?" Clare said, laughing.

As long as my body wasn't in the water, I loved it. I stored it in my memory with all the other streams and lakes and waterfalls.

We stopped in Grand Marais as much to buy fudge and donuts as to stretch our limbs. Paul thought the fudge from Beth's Fudge was the best in the world. Our children agreed with him. I wasn't one to ask since I've never liked chocolate but the best donuts were across the street. That we all agreed on.

Grand Marais was a wonderful town to walk around in, with a variety of shops from Antique Shops to Scandinavian Shops to General Stores. Also, there were many types of restaurants that catered to families.

We browsed the shops and walked down by the marina. The bright reds, greens and yellows of the sails on the sailboats were a contrast to the sky and water. We watched an artist as he tried to copy the changing scene onto his canvas. The setting and the painting were so lovely. I wished, not for the first time, that I could paint more than stick figures.

With several pounds of fudge tucked under Paul's arm, we drove back to Lutsen.

We relaxed the rest of the day and discussed what we should do in the morning. Number one on the list was the alpine slides at Lutsen Mountains.

We were in no hurry the next morning. We let the girls sleep, had a leisurely breakfast, and piled into the van about ten o'clock.

None of us had been on an alpine slide.

They gave us what they called toboggans to carry and we headed for the chair lift. The sleds were heavy for the girls so Paul carried two. One was for Colleen and him, and the other was for Erin.

At the top we waited for each other so we could figure out who was going first. We walked to the beginning of the slides where there were two lanes, a fast one and a slow one.

"C'mon, Oh. You should go in front of me," I said to Erin as I proceeded to the slow lane. Erin had never had a nickname until Colleen started talking. Erin was too difficult for her to pronounce. It came out sounding more like Owen. We had shortened it to Oh.

"I'm following Dad," Erin said. She would be eight years old in October. She had conquered many of the fears she had when she was younger. Even though she still carried her blanket with her, I didn't have a timid little "shadow" anymore. And one thing she had always loved was speed; the faster, the better.

"I am too," Clare said.

"Me too," Anne said.

In my younger days, I was really quite adventuresome. It was hard convincing my girls of that when I moved over into the slow lane. I pictured myself scraping arms and legs along the cement track. Or having the metal runners on the bottom of the sled slice into my exposed flesh. I parted company with the rest of my family.

"Do you think Colleen should go down the fast lane?" I asked no one in particular.

There was no answer.

"Push your glasses up, Coll." I resisted telling her to be careful.

Colleen gave her glasses an upward nudge as she moved over to the fast lane.

Their line was moving along faster than the one I was in. Paul, with Colleen on his lap, went first. Soon they were out of my sight. The other three girls followed in rapid succession.

There were still several people in front of me. I was encouraged that none of them seemed to be taking off like they were shot from a cannon. I watched each and every takeoff until it was my turn.

The boy gave the signal for me to go.

I sat up straight, pushing with my feet, and inched the lever forward to release the brake. I crept along. An incline appeared toward the first turn. Wanting to test my brakes, I pulled back on the lever. They worked well. I could stop completely if I wanted to. I meandered into the first turn. The rear of the sled was swinging back and forth making it hard to keep control. I concluded that I would have better command of the sled if I went a bit faster. I pressed the lever forward again and accelerated. I was fine on the straight section. I approached the second turn. I had to lean into it as I found myself going high onto the curved sides. It was exhilarating.

I didn't want to get reckless and have the sled full throttle the whole run, but neither did I want ten people behind me as I snailed to the end.

I found a medium speed that was perfect for me. I turned a corner and there was a hill with a large sign reading, "DO NOT USE BRAKES ON HILL." The hill went straight down. I hadn't had the chance to slow down before approaching it. I hit the almost vertical hill at a high speed. For a fragment of a second I was airborne. The sled was wobbling all over the track.

Oh, my God, I could've flown off the sled and scraped along the cement on my face, I thought.

In that moment of terror I decided that my body was a delicate entity that could be hurt or easily broken, maybe permanently.

I pulled back on the lever.

I had to pay close attention to every curve until I got to the second hill. DO NOT USE BRAKES ON HILL. I glanced at the sign for a split-second. I paced myself before advancing to the top of the hill. I braked for a second, and then urged the lever forward. The second hill was a piece of cake. One more curve appeared before the finish. As I came out of the final curve, I thrust the lever as far forward as it would go. I wanted my family to think I had been going all out.

The five of them waited for me, holding onto their sleds. They were expecting something that resembled a snail worming to the finish with people lined up behind me, cursing.

I heard one of them say, "Slow down, Mom," as I screeched to a halt for a grand finale.

They looked at each other.

"Did you like it?" Erin asked.

"It was fun."

"Really?" Clare asked.

"Really."

"I can't believe you liked it," Clare said.

"Why? You think I'm a wimp?" I didn't get an answer. I smiled to myself.

"You didn't go that slowly," Paul said.

"I know."

"Want to go again?"

"Sure."

Colleen sat on the chair lift with me to tell me about her exciting ride.

"Were you scared on the hills?" I asked.

"A little."

"Me too."

We went our respective ways, the five to the fast lane on the left while I veered to the right.

"Mom, don't you want to go in the fast lane?"

"No, that's okay." If I could repeat the finish again, I'd be all set.

We had our three rides down and then walked over to the Gondola Rides. While water and speed gave me pause, heights didn't bother me in the least. We went up into the Lutsen Mountains via the gondola. The entire valley was visible with Lake Superior in the distance.

Lutsen was a popular place for snow skiing during the lengthy Minnesota winters. We could see the cleared areas where people skied. There were also long runs over bridges that spanned swiftly moving streams. Even with the many ski runs, the dense evergreen and birch forests covered the mountains.

These weren't mountains like we had seen out West, but, nonetheless, they were beautiful.

We got off at the peak, where a building had food and beverages for sale. We looked through the magnifying telescopes and strolled around the park at the top of the mountain. After a half hour, we were ready to take the gondola back.

Another place that interested us was the Superior Hiking Trail. Although nowhere near as long, it had been patterned after the famous Appalachian Trail. The trail started in Two Harbors, a town about 20 miles north of Duluth. It continued snaking north all the way to Canada, more than 240 miles. Within the Superior Hiking Trail were seven state parks, two national forests, and two state forests. It was a true wilderness filled with moose, deer, bears, and wolves; wildflowers and berries; eagles, hawks, and many other birds; clear inland lakes, waterfalls, tumbling rivers, and streams.

The trails themselves were sometimes no wider than a footpath and the hiking went from easy to treacherous. Some of them went into the higher elevations until the hiker was more than 1500 feet above Lake Superior. Many of the trails were alongside the streams and waterfalls I loved so much.

Since I've always been consistent, I much preferred the easier hikes. Moderate difficulty was also okay. I'd leave the difficult to treacherous hikes to the hiking clubs. Why work up a sweat and make my muscles sore over a hike?

We had a light lunch and settled on the Temperance River Gorge.

We weren't disappointed. The Temperance River roared as it gushed through the gorge. The rocks within the whole area were over a billion years old. We hiked above the gorge to explore further. The actual trail followed the churning river. There were whirlpools of water, overlooks, and people swimming in some of the quieter sections of the river.

"Isn't this wonderful?" I said.

"It's cool," Anne said.

"Yeah, really cool," Clare said.

The girls were tired after about a mile. We turned around because we had to walk the same distance back. We took turns carrying Colleen.

We drove to the hotel.

My book awaited me. I sat by The Lake reading with Paul while our children skipped rocks.

Life didn't get any better than this.

In the van the next morning, we talked about where we would stop on the way home. Paul and I were interested in a place called the Palisade Head.

We turned off the highway at the entrance to the Palisades, a well-known spot for people to stop and take pictures. The road off the main highway was narrow and like a steep corkscrew. It was kind of scary. When we got to the top, the van leveled off and we could park. The six of us got out to see if we wanted to take a picture.

I was incredulous.

We stood on the top of an enormous cliff of sheer rock. The cliff went around the shoreline in the shape of a horseshoe. Far below, the waves broke softly against the sand.

The camera came out and we clicked one picture after another.

"Don't get too close to the edge," I said to the girls. I kept a respectable distance from the brink. All the tightrope and ballet moves I had learned on our trip weren't going to help me if I tumbled over the edge, smashing my head, arms, legs, and torso on the cliff face and rocks below. I'd probably drown in addition to breaking every bone in my body. I noticed my husband pulling the girls back.

"Be careful," he said as he held Colleen's hand.

I walked over to the two of them.

"This is making me nervous," Paul said quietly.

"Me too. Let's go."

We called the other girls and got back in the van.

"Did you guys like it?" I asked.

"Yeah," the four replied in unison.

"I think it's wonderful to look at. Standing on the edge was . . ." I couldn't finish the sentence. I shivered.

"Mom, I thought you liked heights," Clare said.

"Not anymore."

It was sad but the older I got, the more cautious I became. By the time I was 50, I'd be scared of just about everything. If there had only been railings, it wouldn't have bothered me. Or a parachute strapped to my back.

Or Cary Grant waiting to catch me if I slipped.

We arrived in Duluth in time for lunch at Grandma's Restaurant. It was located where the gigantic ore ships came into the harbor. A gong sounded as the middle of the lift bridge ascended to allow the ships to pass. All eyes in the restaurant stared out the windows when the gong sounded. It happened twice during our lunch. We watched, with everyone else, as the lift bridge rose and the ore boats cruised by us.

"They're huge," Anne exclaimed.

"Enormous," Clare said.

"Probably bigger than a whale," Erin said.

"Or an effelent," Colleen said, stumbling over the word.

We talked about the Maritime museum across the street

from the restaurant. Our children had visited the museum before so we didn't walk over. One of the things that intrigued me was the ice cutting boats they used every spring. For the people of Duluth, the harbor ice was a reality for six months of the year. When it started to break up, they had to send the ice cutting boats through before the ore ships could make it.

We talked about the harshness of the winter and what people did in the past without heat, running water, electricity, bathrooms, refrigerators, washing machines, warm Thinsulate clothing, and supermarkets.

They must have been a lot tougher than we were.

During the rest of our two-and-a-half hour drive home we chatted about how much we loved the North Shore.

"It's my favorite place in the world," I said.

Everyone agreed, a true milestone in our family. Consensus had rarely ever happened and it hasn't happened since.

The four girls wanted to return to Lake Superior the next summer. Paul and I did, too.

"We should make it our end of the summer place every year," Anne said.

"Good idea," I said.

I pushed up Colleen's glasses as we walked through the door of our house.

"I love our house," Colleen said.

"I do too." I looked around at my real favorite place in the world. Home Sweet Home.

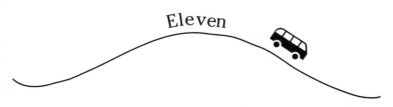

Eleven

Washington, Jefferson, and Lincoln, Oh My

Children need space as they learn about history.

We spent another two winters bundled up under afghans planning what we would do in the summer of 1992. Since we had had so much fun in Canada and the North Shore, we discussed whether we should go back for a week. I brought up the Grand Canyon a couple of times but it didn't illicit much interest from Paul or the girls.

Paul's idea was that we should fly wherever we went and then rent a car. After many discussions, we finally settled on Washington D. C., home of the Smithsonian museums. I blissfully thought about all the museums we would stroll merrily through. I was sure the girls would learn to love them as much as I did. We would bond in our mutual museum interests and talk about what we had seen for years to come.

"Are we going way up in the air?" Six-year-old Colleen asked.

"Just for a short time. Then we'll be in Washington D. C." It never ceased to amaze me that one gets onto a plane and then a few hours later lands in a totally different place.

"How do the planes stay up?" Nine-year-old Erin asked.

"Well, they have wings that help them. The pilot gets the speed up on the runway and we're lifted up." As I was talking and trying to reassure Colleen and Erin that indeed planes do stay up in the air, I realized that I knew little about the dynamics of flying or anything else to do with planes. Really, how did they stay up in the air? I'd have to ask Paul later.

Yellowstone, seven years earlier, had been our last long driving trip. Now that our girls were older, it should be that much easier. Since we had learned so much about traveling with children and how to keep the peace, we didn't hesitate to mark off two weeks on our calendar. I happily told everyone I met about our upcoming trip.

I was sure the mother who kept shuddering, as she recounted their family vacation with two teenagers, was exaggerating. Others said they would never travel with teenagers again.

"The best thing about our vacation was when we got home," one mother stated.

"That was the only good thing about ours," another mother agreed.

I turned my ears off as the two mothers tried to top each other with vacation horror stories. How could it be any harder traveling with three adolescents and a six-year-old than traveling with toddlers and preschoolers?

We arrived in Washington Dulles Airport on an August afternoon ready to take the city by storm. We didn't need a car while we were in Washington, D. C., so we took a cab to the Embassy Suites hotel.

After dropping off our luggage and eating a light supper, we took a night tour of the city. We had already seen the Jefferson Memorial, the Capital, and the Kennedy Center for the Performing Arts when the bus pulled up to the Lincoln Memorial. Darkness was all around while Lincoln was illuminated in his chair. Nighttime made it especially memorable and majestic.

"Do you realize we're standing at the Lincoln Memorial?" I tried to sound the perfect combination of interesting and informative.

"Yes, Mom."

"Do you realize that he grew up in a log cabin?"

"Yes, Mom."

"He never thought he'd be president someday."

"Yes, Mom."

"He's my favorite president."

"We know, Mom."

"Well, maybe one of you will be the first female president."

"God help us all," Paul said.

The next morning we went to the National Museum of American History. We watched as a huge flag was raised to patriotic music. The flag was kept in a controlled environment most of the time to protect the cloth.

"They wrote 'The Star Spangled Banner' about that flag," I said. The immense flag filled a whole wall.

"Even though it's all ripped up?" Clare said. A tape played, giving the history of the flag. We learned that the lower eight feet of the flag had been cut off and given away as souvenirs.

"It didn't start out like that."

"I don't like the paint all over it," Erin said. There was a large white stain on the flag. Perfectionist Erin thought they should have thrown the flag away. "And what's that red V for?"

"We'll have to find out about the white stain," Paul said.

"As you can see there is a large white stain on the flag," the tape intoned. "One of the stars was cut out for a souvenir. The red upside down A, we think, stands for the Armistead family, who donated the flag to the nation."

We finished touring the American History Museum and then went next door to the National Archives building. When we walked up the huge steps, I felt as if I was walking on air. I stopped in front of the gigantic doorway for a few seconds. The sheer size of the doorway dwarfed me as I passed beneath them.

Standing in line, we waited to get a glimpse of the Declaration of Independence. Kept in an environmentally controlled box, it was lowered at night to protect the paper from disintegration.

"C'mon, girls, it's the Declaration of Independence," I said. "Can you believe it?"

Paul went first, followed by the four girls, and then me. I was so thrilled when it was my turn that I felt almost a reverence. This was the beginning of our country. We had studied the Declaration of Independence and the Constitution in school from a young age. I remember my teachers saying, "Our forefathers were very farseeing. They set up a government that would last." I could have gawked all day but there were people lined up behind me.

My girls waited by a glass case with another document in it. Since the line was smaller, I soon saw the reproduction of the Magna Carta. The ornate handwriting crowded the page with swirly letters. I imagined a person hunched over a paper writing with a quill pen.

"What was that document?" Anne asked.

"A copy of a very famous document called the Magna Carta."

"When was it written?"

"In the thirteenth century."

"We weren't here yet."

"It was written in England to try to limit the king's power." I was just getting revved up to talk about the importance of farseeing men in history and how much we should appreciate them.

"Okay," Anne said. She turned and walked out of those magnificent front doors.

I wanted to say "Wait, I wasn't done yet . . ." but she was gone. I wanted to tell her that it had set up our Constitution because no one was above the law. But Anne was out of sight. I looked around for the rest of the family. No luck. I peered out the front door and there they were.

"Well, did you like it?"

"It was okay," Clare said.

"Just okay?"

"I liked it okay."

I questioned no further. It was better that way. We took a break for lunch before going to the Natural History Museum. I knew within a few minutes of walking into the museum that this was a place where I could spend many happy days. Erin circled the huge elephant in the rotunda with a mammoth grin on her face. It was her favorite animal. She circled the elephant for a second time stopping in front of the ample trunk.

"Where's the Hope Diamond?" Anne asked every time we even slowed down in an exhibit. She wanted to make a bee-line for it.

We strolled around the exhibits, enjoying the different cultures, the dinosaurs, prehistoric times, mammals, shark's teeth and jaws.

"Look, Colleen, it's Megamouth. Even a Great White

Shark could fit into its mouth," Clare said. She pointed to the wall where the jaws of sharks hung.

"I like the teeth." Colleen said.

"Not if they bit you, you wouldn't," Erin said.

"Where's the Hope Diamond?" Anne asked.

We went through the display of insects.

"Look at that beetle," Erin exclaimed, pointing at a rhinoceros beetle.

Colleen was intent on the butterfly display. "Do you think it hurts when the pin goes through their head."

"They're already dead, Colleen," Clare explained.

"Just think, they killed them just so they could pin them to a board," Erin had walked over to look.

"Where's the Hope Diamond?" Anne asked.

All of us wanted to see the Hope Diamond so we made our way to the gems and minerals exhibit. Paul and I were fascinated by the entire exhibit which told how the gems formed in the earth as well as how the different colors came to be.

We sauntered over to the display of the Hope Diamond and, there it was, 45 plus carats of clear blue diamond.

"Ooh, pretty," Colleen said.

"Where did they find it?" Clare asked.

"Well, let's see. It was mined in India in the 1600s." I said, reading the history out loud. "King Louis XIV bought it in 1668."

"Did he keep it?" Erin asked.

"It looks like after the French Revolution it was stolen. It reappeared in England in 1812." Paul said.

"Then another king owned it, King George IV of England. After his death it was sold to pay off his debts." I said. "Henry Hope was the next owner."

"That's why it's called the Hope Diamond," Clare said. "How'd the museum get it?"

"It was donated in 1958 by Henry Winston, Inc."

Anne had been reading along with Paul and I. She glanced over at the display again and said, "It isn't THAT great."

"I think it's pretty," Clare said. "It's really blue."

I lifted Colleen so she could see better and Paul lifted up Erin. We ogled for a while and then moved out of the way for others to see.

It was after four in the afternoon when we came out of the museum. What to do next? Paul and I realized that we couldn't see everything with four children along.

The National Gallery of Art stood in front of us. Even though we knew next to nothing about art, Paul and I thought we should at least walk through. The museum beckoned.

"Who wants to see the art museum?" Paul said.

"I do," I said.

"I think we should go back to the hotel," Anne said.

"I do too," Clare said.

Paul sat reading through the brochure. "It sounds kind of neat. They even have Picasso paintings."

Erin and Colleen listened but said nothing. Anne was ready to go back to the hotel; she didn't care what the museum offered. Clare's curiosity was piqued about seeing a Picasso so she quickly changed her mind.

"No, you can't change your mind," Anne said, glaring at Clare.

"I want to see it." Clare moved away from Anne.

"I don't know why. He's weird. And I'm really hot. Can't we go back?"

"I really want to see the Picasso from his early period," Paul said. "We'll walk through and then leave right away. Okay, Anne?"

"I want to go now. This is so boring."

"I want to see Picasso, too," Erin piped up.

"Me too," Colleen said.

"Okay, let's go," Paul said. "It'll be quick, Anne, I promise." We had promised the girls that we would quit by five o'clock every day.

We consulted the map so we could see where the early Picasso hung. Anne held up the rear as the rest of us hustled along. We stopped at several beautiful paintings by Matisse and Rembrandt. We wanted to learn more about them but we had promised to make a bee-line for the early period Picasso and then leave.

"I don't think it's weird at all," Clare stated.

"Well, look at that." Paul moved closer to the painting. "It's wonderful."

"It is wonderful," I said. I resolved then and there to learn more about painting and especially about the early period of Picasso. I couldn't take my eyes off the face looking back at us; it was so beautiful.

Anne had picked up Colleen and they came closer. The six of us made a semi-circle around the painting. We moved around so we could see the details of "The Lady with a Fan."

"Maybe we'll get a chance to come back here another day," Paul said.

"When the kids grow up."

"I'd really like to spend some time here."

"I would too."

Outside again, we walked over to where the cabs waited. Soon we were at the Embassy Suites with our first full day almost over. After eating and swimming, the girls got on their pajamas. Anne and Clare had the hideaway bed in the other room of the suite. They opened up the bed, plopped down on it, and flipped through all the channels on the cable TV again and again and again. The flipping mesmerized Colleen and Erin and soon the four of them were on the bed listening to Anne click the remote control.

We called Erin and Colleen at 9:30 p.m. because they were sleeping in our room. I could have told the other girls to turn off the TV but I knew it would be back on as soon as we left the room. Although Paul and I had no idea what they were watching, we closed the door and let Anne and Clare flip the channels to their heart's content.

"Someday we'll come back and go through the art museum," Paul said.

"Just the two of us?"

"Just the two of us."

We took the subway to Ford's Theater early the next morning.

"Do you realize that this is the place where Lincoln was shot, girls?"

"Yes, Mom."

"Can't you feel it?"

"No," Anne said.

"I don't want to feel it," Clare said.

"I mean the atmosphere. There's a presence," I said.

"You mean there's a ghost here?" Erin said.

"Colleen, there's a ghost. Are you scared?" Anne raised her hands, wiggled her fingers, and moved them towards her six-year-old sister. "Ooooh."

"Mom, is there a ghost?" Colleen asked as she leaned against me.

"There's no ghost," I said to my youngest. "Don't pay any attention to them."

As we walked up the steps to the box seats, there were some ooooh sounds coming behind me.

We went across the street to see where Lincoln had died. I was amazed by how small the bed was. The guide described how Lincoln's six-foot-four inch frame was literally hanging off of the end. I could believe it. It looked as if our six-year-old Colleen would fit in the bed just fine.

Anne pointed at the pillowcase. I looked through the plastic covering. A streak of brown was on the far side.

"As you can see, there is still a little blood on the pillowcase where Lincoln laid his head," the tour guide stated. She continued to talk about the events of that night.

We could imagine how horrible that night was. After

suffering years of Civil War, the nation lost the leader who had worked so hard to preserve it.

I wondered if Lincoln would be surprised just how admired and loved he is generations later.

We walked through the Capital, craning our necks to see every inch of the lovely rotunda. We then stopped at the Air and Space Museum. The Spirit of St. Louis was there as well as the space capsule in which John Glenn orbited the earth. The capsule had so little room that it was hard to imagine any person inside it, much less a grown man.

"Do you realize that John Glenn was actually in there when he went around the earth?"

"Yes, Mom."

"There isn't much room in there. I'd get claustrophobic."

"Me too," Erin said.

Before we left we bought freeze-dried ice cream; the same kind that the astronauts eat. None of us liked it so Colleen began feeding it to the birds. Soon she had a whole group of pigeons and other birds around her. She skipped with a huge smile on her face as the birds followed her. Every few seconds she would toss a handful of ice cream to the birds. They gulped it down. Colleen noticed one bird who wasn't quick enough to get anything. She zeroed in on the timorous bird. It was hard to distract the others but she managed to get food to the little one. The rest of us sat to watch Colleen and cheer the little bird on.

We then walked down to the Washington Monument.

Standing in line for a long half hour did not sit well with Anne. "Can we go? It's hot," she said, scowling.

"It is hot. There's nothing we can do about it," Paul said.

"We could go."

I walked to the back so I didn't have to listen to the complaining. Our turn finally came and we took the elevator to the top of the Monument. We could see the White House, the Pentagon, the Capital, and many other buildings clearly as we looked through the small windows.

We went back to the hotel at five even though the art museum was again beckoning to Paul and me. After we got on our pajamas, I asked the girls to say what their favorite part of the day was.

"Anne, what did you like?" Paul said.

"Nothing," Anne said.

"What do you mean nothing? There has to be something you liked," I said.

"Okay, I liked watching Colleen feed the birds."

"Colleen, what was your favorite thing?"

"I liked everything."

"You can't say that," Anne said.

"I liked feeding the birds the best."

"Clare?" Paul asked.

"I liked the Washington Monument."

"Paul, what about you?" I asked.

"I think it would have to be The Spirit of St. Louis."

"Mom?" Clare asked.

"I can't decide. I loved Ford's theater and the little

house across the street. And I loved the Air and Space Museum."

"You have to pick one."

"Okay. John Glenn's capsule is it."

"How come not something about Lincoln?" Paul asked.

"I don't know. I liked everything. And I really liked watching Colleen feed the birds."

"Can I say I liked the elephant even though we saw it yesterday?" Erin asked.

"Sure."

"Well, then, that's what I liked the best."

To the sound of flipping channels in the other room, I drifted off dreaming of flags, blue diamonds, rotundas, and space capsules.

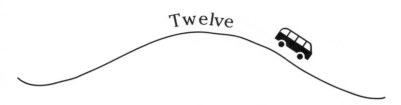

Twelve

Hair, Hips, and Other Shortcomings

Love yourself the way you are
no matter what your children say

During the previous year, things had changed drastically for our oldest daughter. She had become a teenager and finished her first year in Junior High. The change from a small grade school to a huge Junior High had been an adjustment for all of us. In September, a couple weeks after we got home from Washington, D. C., Anne would turn 14 and start the eighth grade. If I had to choose one word to describe her, it would be Cool with a capital C.

According to Anne, everything we saw in D. C. was too hot, too boring, too much history, boring again, not interesting, definitely not cool. The Hope Diamond got a "It isn't THAT great." The Spirit of St. Louis got a "Who's Lindbergh?" The Washington Monument, a "Why don't they have air conditioning?" The Picasso got a corner of one eye with an eyebrow raised and no comment. As the complaints and lack of appreciation went on and on, instead of asking Anne if she liked it, I chose to enjoy it so much that she'd have to love it.

"Wasn't that wonderful?" I said as we came out of the Washington Monument.

Anne's eyes rolled.

"I loved all of it."

"I didn't."

"Your loss."

"I don't think so."

Another change after Anne became a teenager was the extreme interest in her mother, meaning me. I don't mean that she was fascinated by my thoughts, my values, my strong or weak beliefs, or my political leanings. It was my clothes that were taking up so much of her energy.

"Mom?"

"What?"

"Don't you think you should change your shorts?"

"Why? What's wrong with them?" I peered down at my black shorts and pinched the crease I had ironed into them.

"Nothing's wrong with them, I guess." Anne looked my shorts up and down, up and down.

"Then why would I change them?"

"The waist is too high." Anne's brown eyes locked into mine.

"That's where my waist is." I felt the dimple on each side of my body and, sure enough, that was just where my shorts should have been resting.

"It seems kind of high."

"I'm too old to be wearing hip huggers." I saw a fleeting picture of myself at 19. Thank God it was a fleeting image. If it had been longer than a second, I might have become depressed and unable to continue the conversation. I wore hip hugger jeans, skin-tight in the thighs, with bell bottoms coming down from just under the knees. I was Cool with a capital C. I blinked and the image disappeared.

"They'd look better than those," Anne said with total conviction.

"I don't think so." After four children the body goes. Anne should have been thanking me for giving up my body as I helped the four girls come into the world. My hips of the distant past were bony and I'd had a much bigger curve in the waist area. However, as I approached middle age, the indentation became more like a dimple on each side and the iliac crest was covered with flesh. It was definitely much softer.

If I did wear hip huggers now, the size of them would be so enormous that Anne would probably collapse from laughing. At least she'd be laughing though, and if she passed out, we wouldn't be hearing all the complaining.

I pondered going back to my teen years for a few seconds and getting a shorter pair of shorts. Then, thankfully, I saw another image. It was of a middle-aged woman trying to push and shove her flesh into a pair of hip huggers. Kind of like the wicked step sisters in Cinderella trying to work their generous feet into the glass slipper. This was not a pretty sight and definitely not cool.

I simply was not uninhibited enough to pull off wearing the above, all for the sake of a few chuckles and my teenager's approval. Anne would just have to accept my high waist, fleshy hips, and too long shorts. I had to every day of my life.

The other part of me that seemed to intrigue her was my hair. One day, she looked at it from all different directions. I finally couldn't stand it one more second. "What are you looking at?"

"Nothing."

"It doesn't seem like nothing."

"Okay, as long as you asked. It's your hair."

"My hair?"

"Yeah, it's too big."

"What do you mean, too big?" I remembered all those teased hairstyles of the Sixties and mine didn't fit into that category at all.

"It's kind of high in the air."

"You don't know what big hair is, Anne." I was about to explain how some of the girls in my high school ratted their hair, when I was interrupted.

"Yes, I do." Anne looked at me when she said it. I

knew what she was thinking; she didn't have to say it. I found myself smoothing down my already smooth hair and quickly pulling my shorts down a notch. For some strange reason, I felt very nervous about myself.

People were not exaggerating when they relayed stories about traveling with teenagers. It was everything they said it was and more. I remembered how I had dismissed all the mother's horror stories. Now I could stand shoulder to shoulder with them and relay some of my own. We could shudder together.

I hadn't been prepared for the moodiness and lack of interest in places that were so interesting. I hadn't been prepared for the adversarial relationship that developed between parents and teenagers. Preschoolers and toddlers might have poked at each other but they still loved their parents. Friends were of paramount importance to teenagers. And the only place they wanted to be was with their friends. Paul and I needed another wise grandfather to help us.

I looked at my youngest daughter who was smiling and laughing as she skipped along. Suddenly I had the most awful thought. Anne used to be like that. In a short seven years, Colleen would be a teenager. And during those seven years we would always have teenagers. I quickly added on the seven years Colleen would be a teenager and got 14 years of teenagers. Many of those years we would have three.

I groaned inside and gave Colleen a big hug. She still let me. In fact, she hugged back with pure joy.

I told Paul my calculations about our years as parents of teenagers. He appeared frightened for a minute. "You won't have to worry," I said. "They'll be so busy checking out my hair and hips they won't have time to look at you."

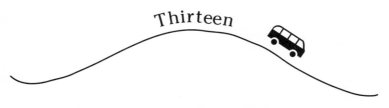

Thirteen

The H Word—History

Each vacation creates a unique family history.

The first night in Washington, D. C., the girls had been shocked by the homeless people sleeping on benches and on the ground. One man covered himself with a newspaper for protection from the elements. It had been misting that night so the poor man had a wet newspaper over his head.

We saw other homeless people walking up and down the mall. They carried or pushed their small amount of possessions. The days were hot and humid but it really cooled down at night. Where did all these people sleep?

"Why are they homeless?" Clare asked.

"Each person has a different story."

"But why?"

"Sometimes they've made bad choices and sometimes they've been very unlucky."

"Don't they get cold?"

"I'm sure they get very cold."

"It doesn't seem fair," Clare said.

"It's not. I don't think anyone should be sleeping on a bench."

"I'd be scared," Erin said.

"Me too." I felt so lucky to be able to take a hot shower and get into a warm, soft bed at night.

"Why don't they do something?" Anne said.

"It's complicated," I said.

"They probably have," Paul said. "We don't know what they've tried."

The discussion came up every day we were in Washington D. C. and we never came up with a good solution.

We wanted to vary what we were doing so the whole two weeks wasn't museums and history. On the third morning we slept in a little, since we planned to spend most of the day at the zoo. Besides, it was hard to arouse Anne and Clare and get them moving. They wanted to stay in bed.

Clare and Anne's late night cable TV watching was taking its toll. The whites of their eyes were pinkish with a roadmap of veins. The two of them moved tortoise-like toward the elevators as we went down for breakfast. Clare kept blinking and rubbing her bleary eyes. Anne yawned and yawned.

"What'd you watch last night?" I asked.

"Just a movie."

"What movie?"

"I don't remember," Anne said. She looked at Clare and something sinister passed between them. It could only mean that they had been watching a movie I would have said no to.

Sometimes I felt as though I was losing all control. As exhausting as little children were, there was nothing devious about them. Teenagers were a whole different breed. I vowed I would coerce the name of the movie out of Clare when we were alone. Then I didn't know what we would do. Paul and I couldn't ban the two of them from watching TV after we went to bed; they'd turn it on anyway. All they'd have to do was wait until we were sound asleep. We wouldn't hear a thing. We would have to come up with some kind of a plan. It was so simple when they were younger; Paul and I just turned off the TV and said, "Time for bed."

Before the zoo, we stopped at the Washington National Cathedral. The open vastness of the space from floor to ceiling was extraordinary. Huge, circular stained glass windows flaunted all the colors in the spectrum. Who designs such magnificence and then makes it come to life? I had to turn in all directions to get the full effect.

And it was so quiet. Even though tours were going through the Cathedral, voices were hushed and reverent. People knelt or sat to pray. A peacefulness surrounded me. I stood in the aisle and I prayed. I prayed for guidance and patience with my children. I prayed not to take their criticisms so personally.

"C'mon, let's go." Anne whispered. "What's SHE doing?"

I didn't have to ask who she was. I hoped the peacefulness I had felt for those few seconds stayed with me throughout my children's teenage years, or at least through the rest of our family vacation. On second thought, maybe the day would be enough to ask for. I would have to take it one long day at a time.

We spent the afternoon strolling around the zoo. We all liked animals so it was pleasant and fun. We joined the large crowd watching the panda bears walk back and forth. Then we meandered over to the elephants. Erin loved watching the elephants get a pedicure and a bath. They dipped their trunks in the water and sprayed it all around.

"Aren't they cute?" Erin asked.

"They're really cute," Paul said.

"Do you think that hurts their feet?"

"No, they don't seem to mind it. The zookeepers have to take care of their nails and feet."

Before we left we stood again to watch the pandas.

After the zoo, we went to the Vietnam Memorial, something Paul and I both wanted to see. Since the Lincoln Memorial was in the same area, we decided to revisit during the daylight hours.

Anne looked around at the Lincoln Memorial. "Haven't we already seen this?"

"We wanted to see it in the daytime," Paul said. He walked into the Memorial holding Colleen's hand.

"And we wanted to see the Vietnam Memorial," I said, following Paul.

"Are we going to be here very long?" Anne asked.

I knew she wanted to be in the hotel channel surfing. I would rather be seeing the wonderful things in Washington D. C. than sitting in the hotel room flipping all the cable channels on the television. Since this was my first time in Washington also, I planned to enjoy every minute of it, past and present.

"I'm going down to the Vietnam Memorial." I gave Lincoln a last gaze and headed down the steps.

"Mom, where are you going?" Anne asked. She had been waiting on the steps for the rest of us.

"To the Vietnam Memorial. Wanna come with me?"

"Maybe."

"Well, c'mon then."

"What about Dad?"

"They'll be coming too."

I pulled down the hem of my shorts, smoothed my hair a couple of times and walked down the steps towards the Vietnam Memorial. Paul and the other girls caught up to Anne and me by the time we reached it.

"Did you know that an architecture student designed this?" I asked.

"Really?" Anne said.

"Really. Her name was Maya Ling Yin and she was only 21."

"Wow."

A large ledger was filled with the 58,000 names

engraved on the Memorial. The brother of one of the girls I went to high school with died in Vietnam when we were Juniors. I located his name and found the section on the Memorial.

As I walked next to the 493 foot long Memorial, people cried, people touched the black granite stone and rubbed the names with their fingers, people transferred the names onto paper with pencil lead, and people stood trying to take it all in. I fell into the latter category. I couldn't quite take it all in.

I found the name I was looking for but suddenly I felt like an intruder. After all, I hadn't known the young man. He had died so far away from home and left people who loved him. This was true of each of the names on the Memorial. They were people who had dreams that would never be realized because they had died for their country. I felt saddened as I walked away.

Clare was standing by Paul. "It's too sad," she said.

"It sure is," I said.

To the strains of "Do we have to go?" by our two TV watchers, we rousted Anne and Clare out of bed at 7:00 a.m. the next day. Clare blinked continuously trying to focus her eyes. Anne put her hand up to her mouth to stifle a nonstop yawn. Neither one said a word as we nudged them towards the front door of the hotel. We had to be at the Washington Monument by eight o'clock to board the bus for Mount Vernon.

Our tour guide talked as we rode through the Virginia

countryside. Paul enjoyed these tours as much as I did. The guide flavored the landscape in such a way that it was easy for me to picture George Washington riding high on his horse as he went back and forth to Mount Vernon. This was no small feat as the cars and buses whizzed past.

We took our time touring Mount Vernon; walking through the house and the other buildings on the property. A wonderful porch stretched across the entire back of the house. Large, black wooden chairs sat comfortably on the porch. They faced out to the green rolling lawn and the Potomac River. Paul and I started to walk along the lawn to take pictures as the girls took up position on the chairs.

"Mom, she hit me," Clare said, pointing at Anne. Paul and I turned around in time to see Anne pushing Clare away from her. She didn't want Clare sitting next to her. Erin poked at Colleen who was trying to get herself up in the huge chair. Colleen shrieked. People stared at our children as they gave each other dirty looks. The girls tried to move as far away from each other as they possibly could. I didn't blame the people, I was staring at our children, too.

Paul and I closed in on the girls.

"She hit me. Aren't you going to say anything?" Clare was indignant.

"Of course I'm going to say something. Anne, knock it off," Paul said.

Anne looked at Paul and said, "When's the tour over?"

Colleen said, "What about Erin?"

"Erin, don't poke Colleen. In fact, all of you keep your hands off each other. Just leave each other alone."

"But I didn't dooo anything. Why am I being yelled at?" Clare said.

Some things never change. The thought was not a comfort as I recalled our driving into Yellowstone. I cringed when I realized we were starting the driving portion of our trip the next day. Nine more days. Nine more days.

Seven years previously the main problem was in the van; once that was resolved, things went smoothly. The main problem this time around was not the long drives, but the fact that one of our children simply did not want to be with any of us. She wanted to be with her friends.

We decided to go down in the direction of the other buildings on the property, separating our children from each other as we walked along. It worked for a short time, but after a while, we were just trying to kill time until the tour left. I was so busy keeping my body between our various children that I don't remember much of anything about that part of the tour.

As we rode back on the bus, we all looked out the window. We still had a tour of Arlington Cemetery and I was getting the idea that no one wanted to go on it. Suddenly, I had an awful thought. Maybe our girls were historied out already. What were we going to do for the rest of our trip?

"Paul, I think they're sick of historical places," I whispered. I didn't want to talk too loud just in case I was wrong and I would be giving them ideas. Actually when I thought about it, I didn't give my children too many ideas; they came up with them just fine on their own.

"I think so too."

"What should we do?"

"There's nothing we can do. It's already planned."

"I'm glad we're not going to Monticello."

"Me too."

We had decided that we should drive down to Virginia Beach instead of Monticello. It would give us a break from the museums and tours that Paul and I loved. The girls could swim and relax on the beach. Everyone would be so happy.

First though, we had to make it through the tour of Arlington Cemetery. We got on a tram bus and the tour guide began. Whatever the girls thought was their own business as they all looked out the windows.

We stopped at the Tomb of the Unknown Soldier to watch the changing of the guard. I stood off by myself, so I wouldn't have to see if anyone didn't like it, or found it boring. I liked the reverence of the soldiers towards the place. I stood a little straighter as I watched the posture of the soldiers.

We got out again when we came to John F. Kennedy and Bobby Kennedy's gravesites. Paul and I remembered those two days of their deaths as we had many times before.

The girls asked us a few questions about it but by the time we got back on the tram, I felt really exhausted.

"What should we do now?" Paul asked.

"Let's go back to the hotel," I said.

"It's not even five."

"I know but I'm really tired."

When we stepped into the hotel room, the phone started ringing. We couldn't imagine who would be calling us. I answered the phone and then handed the receiver to Clare. It was a boy who had been down at the pool every night. He wanted eleven-year-old Clare to meet him there.

"Absolutely not," Paul said.

"Why not?" Clare asked. She held the phone away from her ear.

"Because you are 11 years old and eleven-year-olds don't date. Would you hang up the phone please?"

"I have to go," Clare said. She hung up the phone, sat down on the couch, and waited.

"Where are his parents?" Paul said while pacing in front of the TV.

Anne moved her neck back and forth trying to see around Paul. "Dad, I can't see the TV."

Paul spun around. "Shut it off, then. On second thought, I'll shut it off." He strode over and turned the TV off.

Anne had never considered that the TV could be off when we were in the hotel room. She didn't quite know what to do with herself, so she gaped at the dark, silent screen.

I was getting a pretty clear idea of what the dating years were going to be like. Boys on the scene, in combination with our teenagers checking out my hair and my total lack of style in clothing, were going to make for some less than harmonious times. As I fenced comments about my person, Paul would be grilling the girls about any boys who came their way.

This sneak preview made me think warily of the future. If there was a way of fastforwarding the next ten plus years, I would surely be interested. Or even going back in time when a story at bedtime and a hug and kiss took care of so much. We were once again in unmarked territory.

"Dad, the parents are going to be there," Clare said.

"Oh," Paul said. "Are you sure?"

"Yes, I'm sure."

"I still don't want you going down there by yourself. Anne or I will go with you."

"Okay."

"And don't make this a habit. Meeting some boy. Understand?"

"Dad, we're leaving tomorrow. I'll never see him again."

"Good." Paul looked delighted at the prospect.

The other girls and Paul went downstairs with Clare to swim. I had a lot of laundry to do before I could pack for the next day. I enjoyed the quiet while washing and folding clothes. After I finished putting the clothes in piles, I went to the pool area to watch my husband and girls.

The next morning we took a cab to Dulles airport to pick up our rental car. Paul handed each girl a roll of nickels, and we drove east towards Maryland. Then we would take a highway going south all the way to Virginia Beach.

As with South Dakota, Yellowstone, and Lake Superior, the whole family wished we had more time in Washington. What a great city! We hadn't seen the White House, the FBI building, the U.S. Mint, and so much more.

Maybe we'll be lucky enough to go back someday.

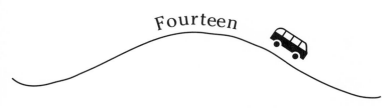

Fourteen

Beachballs and Boys

Growing pains can be confusing for
both adults and children

With nickels working their magic on our children, I could enjoy the breathtaking scenery of Chesapeake Bay. Anne and the others looked out the windows, thinking their own private thoughts, but at least they weren't battling each other. No remote control was being clicked either. The respite was more than welcome.

Before pulling up to Virginia Beach, we wanted to stop at Jamestown, one of the first settlements of the immigrant Europeans. It interested Clare and Erin but not Anne. She decided to sit on the bench with Colleen outside the little fort.

A replica of the tiny ship lay moored in the water. We walked through the vessel, wondering how people survived the voyage itself. I imagined storms tossing the ship side to side and the sounds of pelting rain, squealing wind, and creaking boards. I imagined fear in the darkness of night.

As we walked out of the ship, we glanced over at Anne and Colleen, who sat on the bench staring off into space. Anne's mouth moved when she saw us, probably asking when we were going to leave. We just waved pleasantly in their direction while walking towards the settlement. I didn't look back.

The settlement was a replica of the original but it gave an idea of what life was like in the 1600s. This was the place of John Smith and Pocohantas. I had always loved reading those stories.

"How long ago was it here?" Clare asked.

"Let's see. It looks like it began in 1607 with 105 people from England. Oh, my gosh, only 38 survived the first year," I said.

"Then, more people came so by 1609 there were 500 people," Paul said.

"That's a lot in the little fort," Erin said.

"The frigid winter of 1609–1610 was called the "Starving Time," Paul read to Erin and Clare. "There were only 60 people left in the spring. Jamestown was abandoned."

"I wouldn't have liked to live here," Clare said.

"Me either. I don't think we would have survived," I said.

"That wasn't the end of it," Paul said. "Leaders in England ordered the settlers back."

"Then, what happened?" Erin asked.

"Well, then, they started to grow tobacco," Paul explained. "The settlement grew to 4500 people in 1623."

As it often does, the human spirit amazed me. To think that these people left their homelands, and most saw neither their country nor their families again. How lonely and sad, yet they continued on to make Jamestown the first permanent settlement.

We walked out of the fort with Clare and Erin still asking questions. We picked up our oldest and youngest at the bench and got back into the car. Our next stop was Virginia Beach.

"It's the ocean, Colleen," Anne said. "Look."

"It's big."

"No, Colleen, it's huge," Clare said. "It's bigger even than Lake Superior."

"Dad, can we get into our swimming suits right away?" Erin asked.

"Sure. But we need to bring in the luggage first."

Everyone grabbed their luggage and dragged them into the room. The suite had two bedrooms and a television room with a pullout couch. With a thud of her suitcase landing, Anne seized the couch. "This bed's mine," she said. She clutched the remote control and rifled through the channels.

We explored the other rooms. Erin and Colleen were in one room while Paul, Clare, and I were in the other. The girls punched their pillows, then plopped onto their beds testing the mattresses for firmness. Clare argued about sleeping in the same room with Paul and me but we wouldn't budge. She would have her own bed and, hopefully, get some sleep. Paul and I had decided that we had to separate Anne and Clare whenever possible at bedtime. That way, only Anne would come home to tell everyone at school and on our block about the exciting movies she had watched. When Anne discovered she'd be sleeping alone, she was happy as a clam, remote control in hand.

I retrieved swimming suits from the suitcases. We changed and the six of us hurried down to the ocean.

"C'mon, Colleen. Let's go," Erin said. "I can't wait."

"I'm coming." Colleen ran as fast as she could.

The four girls gingerly placed their feet in the water and slowly walked up to their knees. As the waves came in their rhythm, the girls jumped over them. The water in the swimming area stayed shallow for a long way so it was perfect for little kids. The three older girls surrounded Colleen to make sure she didn't go too deep.

Anne's eyes darted around checking out the people on the beach. Her eyes settled on a group not too far from us. I followed her eyes, found who she was interested in, and elbowed Paul. His eyes followed mine and the color left his face. A group of boys stood surveying the beach. They looked at Anne, poked each other, and looked again. Two of them ambled over to the sand directly in front of the girls. An interplay proceeded between these two and our oldest. It consisted of eyes locking, then looking down coyly, then locking again.

Soon the boys were walking into the water and Anne had a smirk on her face. She didn't move any closer to them; she knew she didn't have to.

In no time, the two boys and Anne were talking. Anne became more and more animated as the three of them talked. I didn't have to worry about eavesdropping; Erin did that just fine. We had used her listening ability more than once in the past year to find out what Anne and Clare were up to. Whatever the girls were doing, if Erin knew about it, she would tell. Kind of like Cousin Sid in *The Adventures of Tom Sawyer.* I wasn't proud of listening to Erin tattle, but in this case, we had to use the resources at hand. The absence of gray areas in Erin's world made her the perfect spy if we needed one. That was Erin, almost ten and living in her own black and white world of right and wrong.

"Why did those two come over here?" Paul said.

"I think you know why."

"Yes, I do and that's what I'm afraid of."

Paul seemed to have an inordinate amount of fear when it came to boys. As much as he thought I overreacted to Anne's comments about my physical appearance, he overreacted far more to even the prospect of boys. It made me wonder about him as a teenager.

As far as I was concerned, Anne and the two boys were talking to each other innocently enough. She was far too young for dating and we were leaving in two days. What could happen in two days? As I pondered that question, I became uneasy. Then I remembered our backup, Erin. My nerves relaxed.

After fifteen minutes, the boys left. We stayed at the beach for another hour until dinnertime. Anne was no-where near as animated at the table with family as she had been earlier. We tried to find out about her visitors on the beach but she wasn't talking.

When we returned to the hotel room, Anne seemed disinterested in the TV. She stayed in the bathroom for a long time. When she emerged, with eye shadow and flut-tery lashes, she walked over to the door.

"Where are you going?" Paul asked.

"Down to the beach." Anne's foot kept the door to our hotel room ajar. Her right hand was on the doorknob and her left hand was on her hip.

"To swim? We don't feel like swimming right now."

"That's okay. I'm meeting some people to play volleyball."

"Who are you meeting?"

"Some people I met."

"Are you meeting those two boys?"

"Them and others. They're not the only ones playing. It's a big group."

"I don't like it at all."

Anne stood there waiting and finally said, "Are you saying I can't even play volleyball with kids my own age?"

"No. that's not what I'm saying. I'm saying that you could play with some girls."

"There'll be girls there too."

"Maybe your sisters could play."

Anne had had it. "So, when I'm on vacation, I can't do

anything with people my own age. I'm just supposed to hang out with my younger sisters all the time and my parents. Why did you even bring us to the beach if I can't have any fun?" she yelled.

"Close the door, please," Paul said tersely. "The whole hotel can hear you."

Anne closed the door but she wasn't done. "I have to spend two weeks not even talking to my friends. Then I can't even look at people my own age. I want to go home."

"We can't go home now."

"I'm never coming on a family vacation again."

By this time I was thinking that I wouldn't be going on another family vacation, either. But I also thought that Anne did have a point. She should be able to spend time with people her own age. I tried to get Paul's attention as he paced from room to room. I finally followed him.

"Paul, wait, I want to talk to you."

"Okay."

"Anne does have a point." I was sure everyone was listening to us but there was no place to go. I suppose we could have gone into the bathroom and closed the door but, somehow, that seemed too strange. I settled for our bedroom area. There was no door so we would have to have our discussion with four sets of ears tuned to every word.

"What are you saying?"

"I'm saying there's nothing wrong with a group of kids playing volleyball. It seems innocent enough."

"Nothing's innocent with teenage boys."

This wasn't the time to ask questions about the past. I had to focus on the present. "We'll just tell her what time to be back," I said.

Paul wasn't convinced yet so I left the room. He would think about it and come out. The girls sat on Anne's couch bed watching TV. I sat down heavily in a chair. Suddenly I felt as if I could go to bed for the night even though it was only seven-thirty.

Paul came out and walked over to Anne. "I want you back here by nine-thirty at the latest."

"Okay, I will be." Anne leapt up and was out the door. She didn't want to take any chance that Paul would change his mind.

He went down to the beach to check on Anne twice in the two hours she was gone. She was back by nine-thirty on the button.

The next day Paul rented a jet-ski. Everyone took their turns riding behind him. When Paul and Erin went about 200 yards away from the beach, dolphins swam alongside them. In the afternoon the waves were choppier and much higher. We soon discovered the reason why. A hurricane was brewing off the coast of Florida. Hurricane Andrew.

We stayed at Virginia Beach all day, relaxing. That night, Anne went down to the beach again to play volleyball. Both Paul and I walked by the area where the kids played volleyball at different times. I had Erin in tow with me alert for any stray words. Luckily, she didn't hear anything that made me think that I had to rush in and save my firstborn.

Anne wanted to stay in Virginia Beach for the rest of the trip. She was quiet the next morning as we drove towards Williamsburg.

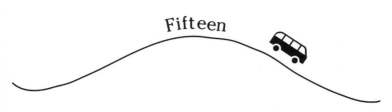

Fifteen

Last But Not Least— Niagara Falls

God's creations are the best of all

We drove around southern Virginia, stopping at Norfolk Naval yard and the Yorktown battle-field. Anne stayed in the car with Colleen as we walked around the battlefield. In this last major battle of the Revolutionary War, General Cornwallis of England was defeated. The scope and size of the battlefield surprised Paul and me. As we looked out on the quiet fields, it was hard to believe that men had fought and died there.

We had talked about going to the water park in Williamsburg one of the two nights we would be there. I had so much laundry to do that I wanted to get it done right away. We ate supper and I took off with a garbage bag full of dirty clothes. I thought if I got it done quickly enough, we could still go. It was after eight o'clock when I got back; too late to start out for the water park.

The next day we went to the area of the city that was known as Colonial Williamsburg. Walking through the houses gave us a sense of the colony of Virginia before the revolution. There was a tavern where the fiery speeches of revolution were spoken.

"Give me liberty or give me death," a man shouted with fist raised above his head.

"Mom, is that supposed to be Patrick Henry?" Clare asked.

"Yes."

"Is this really where they talked about Revolution?" Anne asked. "I don't believe that it was this exact spot."

"That's what it says."

People in the houses and exhibits dressed in period costumes and they stayed in character when asked questions. Other historical figures could be heard giving speeches on the street corners. Blacksmiths, haberdashers, and pharmacists plied their trades.

We stood in line at the Governor's Mansion for a tour. We saw the living quarters of the governor and his family as well as where the cook and laundress toiled all day every day. The cook actually had some fish for us to try and some cookies. We walked around the sculptured gardens in the back of the house.

"Isn't this neat?" I asked.

"Mm, hmm," Erin said.

"I like the garden," Colleen said, while skipping along.

We tried to stay together but it wasn't always easy with the crowds of people. Paul and I turned around constantly to make sure that the four girls were with us. Anne or Clare hung on to Colleen's hand wherever we went.

"You don't have to worry about losing Mom," Clare said to Erin. "You just look for the big hair." They both nodded.

I had turned halfway around when I heard my name. I couldn't believe my ears. The idea of my big hair had filtered down to my two middle children. I licked my fingers and ran them from scalp to the ends of my hair, trying to flatten it. "Wait a minute," I said. "Do you really think that my hair is big?"

Clare and Erin looked at each other, at my hair, and then back at each other.

"Yeah, Mom, it's big," Clare said.

"Yeah, really big," Erin said.

I felt self-conscious, picturing my hair towering above a crowd as we moved along. I nudged Paul with my elbow. "Do you think I have big hair?"

"Don't pay any attention to what they say," he said. "Your hair is fine."

I felt better but I resolved to look in women's magazines for a new hairstyle. On the other hand, why should I change my appearance because my girls commented on it? I walked along, head held high, high above the crowd. The only problem was that from my vantage point, I could everyone's hairdo. I kind of crouched down as I walked and stared straight ahead.

The girls were interested in the wooden stocks that were used for punishment. Clare and Erin each put their faces and hands in them. The wooden upper piece held them in place.

"Mom, you do it," Clare said.

"Yeah, Mom, it's fun," Erin exclaimed.

"Okay, I'll try it." I placed my neck into the spot for the head. It wasn't too bad until I tried to put both wrists in their dug out spots. The position was so uncomfortable that I could only put one hand in its place.

"Let's lock her in there," Clare said as she closed the upper piece over my head and one hand. "Ha ha."

How quickly they turn on you. "Get me out of here," I said. "Now." Clare lifted the wooden piece up and my head and hand were free.

Clare went running over to Paul. "Did you get a picture?"

"No, I didn't. I wasn't quick enough."

"Thank God," I said. Two years earlier, as I catapulted out of the waterslide, my picture had been snapped. The sad little photograph was our children's favorite item to bring to "show and tell." From now on, I'd have to look around for cameras before doing anything.

Rain started about four in the afternoon just as we were getting ready to leave for the water park. It showed little sign of letting up, so we went for an early dinner. We ate at a leisurely pace, hoping the rain had stopped, but we came out of the restaurant to cloudy skies. As the rain pelted our car, thunder rumbled like a timpani drum, and lightning sprinted across the sky.

We drove back to the hotel. The girls were disappointed. Every so often they looked out the window hoping the rain had stopped. About seven o'clock, the rain slowed to a fine mist, and we decided to go to the park. The girls hustled around the almost empty park and flew down as many slides as they could. This continued until we heard the intercom signaling the closing of the park.

The next morning we drove along the western edge of Washington, D. C. and then north towards Pennsylvania. A short distance over the border, we arrived in Gettysburg, Pennsylvania where the battle of Gettysburg took place in 1863. Around the town were interesting little novelty shops. I noticed a wonderful Irish shop near the hotel so I asked Anne if she wanted to come shopping with me.

"I'll buy you a Claddaugh ring for your birthday," I said. I had worn a Claddaugh ring from the time of my 27th birthday. The girls knew the rings had to be given to you by someone else. Mine had been given to me by Paul. The famous design has hands that stand for friendship, a crown that stands for loyalty, and a heart that stands for love.

"Really?"

"Really. Let's look at what they have."

Anne zeroed in on the ring display. She tried on several silver rings until she found the perfect fit.

"We'll take it," I said. I paid the woman behind the counter.

"Thanks, Mom," Anne said. She looked down at her finger as we walked.

"You're welcome."

We stopped in the Visitor Information Center to find out our options for touring the battlefield. There were licensed guides available or a car tape which gave an audio tour. We settled on the car tape which proved to be a good choice. The tape offered background on the battle and told the driver where to turn. It was a fascinating way to learn about the three day battle. Also, the audience was truly captive which helped our children keep their interest.

We stopped the tape many times and got out to walk around. Again, we were amazed by the size and scope of the battlefield. Over 40 miles of roads and 5700 acres of fields are within the grounds. Looking out on the quiet green fields as we had at Yorktown, it was hard to imagine that 51,000 people had died there.

We saw Little Round Top and the spot where the ill-fated Picket's Charge took place. We stood in front of the Minnesota memorial and read inscriptions on some of the other monuments found there. After we finished the driving tour, we visited the Battle of Gettysburg Information Center to look at the uniforms, muskets, and other Civil War memorabilia.

We had one more stop to make before going back to the hotel. The girls wanted to see it too, so we heard no complaints as we drove towards the graveyard where Lincoln gave the Gettysburg Address. I could picture our sixteenth president standing at the podium delivering his speech.

"This is where Lincoln gave his famous speech, girls," I said.

"Which one was that?" Clare asked.

"Let's see. Maybe it was the Gettysburg Address since we're in Gettysburg," Anne said.

"Oh, yeah."

All of us stood behind the podium and looked out at the graveyard. I'm sure Lincoln had a sad, heavy heart as he walked through the freshly dug graveyard. We all did, almost 130 years after the battle. It was an eerie place.

The next day we had a full day of driving as we drove north towards Niagara Falls, our last stop on our family vacation. We were in for a treat though, as we drove through the Appalachian Mountains. The mountains re-minded me of the Bighorns in Wyoming. I exclaimed as I had in the Bighorns at the splendor before us.

"I had no idea the Appalachians were so gorgeous," I said.

"They're really beautiful," Paul agreed.

We could hear the Falls bellowing before we saw them. The windows were rolled down and our necks were craned as we tried to see Niagara. We drove across the bridge that spanned the Niagara River and we had a full view of the Horseshoe Falls.

"I see it."

"I do too."

"Let me see."

"Look at all that water."

"Where does it go?"

"It's so loud."

It was indeed loud as Niagara literally roared its power. We had to check in at the hotel before going down to the Falls. The girls were so excited that they didn't seem to care where they would be sleeping, or with whom.

"Hurry up."

"Let's go."

"Yeah, let's go."

Our hotel was on the Canadian side right next to the Horseshoe Falls. We walked down the steps and over to the rail where people stood. The rail was about three feet high, and if I had bent over at the waist, I could have touched the water. There, Niagara plunged 173 feet in a gushing water flow of 212,000 cubic feet per second. I thought the rail should have been at least chest high, so I stepped back a foot or two. I pictured myself going over and landing with a thud on the rocks below. Even Cary Grant couldn't have saved me!

"Cool. This is really cool," Anne said with a gigantic smile. She hung on tightly to Colleen as they peered over the rail.

"It is cool," I said. I guess it took one of God's creations to wow our teenage daughter. We stood mesmerized by the sound, the sight, and the smell of the 6600 tons of water per second cascading into spray and mist. We looked across the river and saw the American Falls as well as the Bridal Veil Falls.

We spent the next day seeing the Falls from every angle. We walked in a tunnel under the Falls, looked out on the wall of water, and listened to the low-pitched creaking. We donned our blue slickers and took a Maid of the Mist boat tour. We drove over on the United States to gaze at the Horseshoe Falls from the American side, and we went back to Canada to gaze at the American Falls.

Newlyweds and older couples strolled arm and arm. Parents pushed their children in strollers or held their hands, while pointing at the Falls. Wherever anyone walked, their eyes were drawn to the magnificent, magical Niagara Falls.

Paul wanted to take a helicopter ride over Niagara to see it from the air. The six of us crammed into the machine and put on headphones. As we lifted off, a tape told us about the Niagara River, the Falls, and the geology of the region.

It would have been really interesting but I was, what only can be described as, terrified. As I watched the pilot, I noticed his hands and feet were moving constantly to keep the helicopter straight and steady. I hoped he had had very good training when he went to helicopter school.

"I like this, don't you, Clare?" Erin asked.

"The liftoff was cool when we went straight up in the air."

"You could barely feel us lift off," Anne said. "It was gentle."

We flew up the Niagara River on our way to the Falls. It was quite a view but I wished I was on solid ground. When we got closer to the Falls, the pilot turned the helicopter sideways so that the ground looked diagonal. We hovered over the Horseshoe Falls for what seemed to be forever. As the pilot turned again, the water became diagonal.

"Look, there's the Bridal Veil," Colleen exclaimed. "Dad, take more pictures."

"I will," Paul said. Paul was busy with the video camera trying to capture every view.

I closed my eyes and prayed it would be over soon. We flew back down the river on our way to the helicopter pad. When we landed, I felt like kissing the ground.

Anne didn't turn on the TV that night. "What was your favorite part of today, Dad?"

"The helicopter, I think."

"Erin, what was yours?" Anne asked.

"I liked walking underneath the Falls. It was groaning."

"Colleen?"

"I loved the Bridal Veil."

"Clare?"

"I loved the Maid of the Mist. That was cool even though we kept getting sprayed in the face."

"Mom, what'd you like best?"

"I bet it was the helicopter," Erin said.

"Yeah, you weren't hanging on too tight," Clare said. Clare clenched her hands on the arms of the chair.

"Well, it wasn't the helicopter. And you're lucky I wasn't hanging onto you. I just like the Horseshoe Falls. That's my favorite."

"Anne, what did you like?" Paul asked.

"I can't pick."

"You have to," Clare said.

"I loved the Maid of the Mist, going underneath, the helicopter, all the different Falls. I loved it all."

That night we went up to a room near the top of the hotel where we could watch a laser light show over the Falls. It was spectacular.

In the morning, we went down to the Falls again before we left for the Buffalo airport.

"Goodbye, Niagara Falls," Clare said as we drove over the bridge.

"Goodbye."

"Goodbye."

Anne just stared at the water, not wanting to leave. She had a smile on her face, maybe committing the scene to memory like I was doing. She couldn't get enough of Niagara.

The plane we flew back to the Twin Cities was smaller than the one we had taken two weeks before. Everything was fine until we hit turbulence. The wind tossed us back and forth, up and down, like a paper airplane. Paul and I grabbed each other's hands and squeezed. Over the intercom the pilot said that the turbulence would be continuing for awhile. I hung onto Paul on my right side and gripped the armrest on my left. My heart palpitated in what I was sure were irregular heartbeats.

"This is great. It's just like a rollercoaster," Colleen said gleefully.

"This is fun," Erin, our speed demon, agreed.

I decided then and there to honor that old adage, "If you can't beat 'em, join 'em." WHEEE!